D0775489

THE
LORD'S SUPPER

FIVE VIEWS

Edited by

Gordon T. Smith

With contributions by

Brother Jeffrey Gros, John R. Stephenson,
Leanne Van Dyk, Roger E. Olson
and Veli-Matti Kärkkäinen

IVP Academic

An imprint of InterVarsity Press
Downers Grove, Illinois

InterVarsity Press
P.O. Box 1400, Downers Grove, IL 60515-1426
World Wide Web: www.ivpress.com
E-mail: email@ivpress.com

©2008 by Gordon T. Smith

All rights reserved. No part of this book may be reproduced in any form without written permission from InterVarsity Press.

InterVarsity Press® is the book-publishing division of InterVarsity Christian Fellowship/USA®, a student movement active on campus at hundreds of universities, colleges and schools of nursing in the United States of America, and a member movement of the International Fellowship of Evangelical Students. For information about local and regional activities, write Public Relations Dept., InterVarsity Christian Fellowship/USA, 6400 Schroeder Rd., P.O. Box 7895, Madison, WI 53707-7895, or visit the IVCF website at <www.intervarsity.org>.

Scripture quotations, unless otherwise noted, are from the New Revised Standard Version of the Bible, *copyright 1989 by the Division of Christian Education of the National Council of the Churches of Christ in the USA. Used by permission. All rights reserved.*

Design: Cindy Kiple
Images: Courtesy of Ken Barton

ISBN 978-0-8308-2884-5

Typeset by The Livingstone Corporation <www.LivingstoneCorp.com>.

Printed in the United States of America ∞

green press INITIATIVE *InterVarsity Press is committed to protecting the environment and to the responsible use of natural resources. As a member of Green Press Initiative we use recycled paper whenever possible. To learn more about the Green Press Initiative, visit http://www.greenpressinitiative.org*

Library of Congress Cataloging-in-Publication Data

The Lord's Supper: five views/edited by Gordon T. Smith; with
contributions by Brother Jeffrey Gros . . . [et al.].
     p. cm.
 Includes bibliographical references and indexes.
 ISBN 978-0-8308-2884-5 (pbk.: alk. paper)
 1. Lord's Supper. I. Smith, Gordon T., 1953- II. Gros, Jeffrey,
1938-
BV825.3.L67 2008
234'.163—dc22
                    2008017363

P	21	20	19	18	17	16	15	14	13	12	11	10	9	8	7	6	5	4	3	2	1
Y	25	24	23	22	21	20	19	18	17	16	15	14	13	12	11	10	09	08			

CONTENTS

INTRODUCTION

For several years I have been teaching the course "The Meaning of the Sacraments" at Regent College in Vancouver, and I have often wished for what you have in your hands: a concise summary of distinctive perspectives on the Lord's Supper, written by those who hold these views and with responses by these same authors to the views of others. And now we have it. I am confident that this will be a valuable resource for those who want to learn more about the Lord's Supper and, in particular, to make sense of the diversity of views regarding this central event in the life of the church.

How better to do this than by listening to those who represent each view? If we want to learn how others regard the Lord's Supper, then we need a format that allows each perspective to be represented by someone who holds that view. As the instructor in the class, I can summarize the diverse views for the benefit of my students. How much more enriching to have them listen to someone who truly represents the view under discussion!

There is no doubt that on this important topic—the Lord's Supper—we have some quite strong differences of opinion. That is evident in the essays gathered here. What is vital, then, is that we express our differences only after we have first attended to the other presenter, that we provide a rejoinder only after we have listened well. These essays are offered in the hope not so much that readers' minds will be changed but that there can, at least, be new understandings: that we will better appreciate the views of the other, that we will learn from the other.

One of the challenges for a collection such as this is that even within each of the five views included, there is significant diversity of opinion. We have identified each of the views as *the* respective perspective—representing the Reformed, Baptist, Lutheran, Roman Catholic and Pentecostal views. But as Roger Olson observes in his essay, there is no single "Baptist" view, so much so that one can genuinely ask if it is even possible to characterize a "Baptist" view, given the diversity of opinion within this camp. While this is especially the case with the view presented by Professor Olson, in some respects this could be said about the other views as well—though perhaps least so with the Roman Catholic view, which has a more centralized doctrinal tradition. But in each case, it is important to keep in mind that the author of the essay is speaking representatively and individually from the perspective with which they are identified—ideally, in a manner that acknowledges some diversity of opinion within that tradition.

Representatives from five theological traditions speak here about the meaning of the Lord's Supper from within that tradition, whether Roman Catholic, Lutheran, Reformed, Baptist or Pentecostal. Some readers may feel a little overwhelmed to read that there are five views—and in many respects, five quite different views. And others will immediately recognize that there are voices not included in this collection: what of the Orthodox, Anglican-Episcopalian, Methodist, and perhaps also the Disciples of Christ, African American and other perspectives? And this is a fair question; indeed, when one of the contributors to this volume submitted his essay, he wondered whether there should not be a sequel: "Five (More) Views of the Lord's Supper"!

Unfortunately, considering additional views in this collection, having more views at the table, would make this into a cumbersome project. Some limit had to be set. We hope that a majority of readers will find this volume helpful in providing at least these views as an aid to understanding their own tradition and as an aid to a greater appreciation of the views of others with whom they might be in conversation on this topic.

As the editor, I felt it particularly important to include the Pentecostal view—as a recognition of the explosive growth of the Pentecostal church movements of the past century.[1] This growth has been matched by an

---

[1] See the comment of Vinson Synan, for example, in *The Holiness-Pentecostal Tradition: Charismatic Movements in the Twentieth Century* (Grand Rapids: Eerdmans, 1997), p. xi, where he observes

emerging Pentecostal theology in the last few years that needs to be both acknowledged and heard—so that those within Pentecostal churches can strengthen their own understanding of the Lord's Supper, and that those of other traditions can better appreciate the emerging voices of Pentecostal theologians.

And this is our objective for all five views: for each essay, we are seeking understanding not merely of the Lord's Supper but also of the views and perspectives of the other, traditions other than our own. And for this, we urgently need to move beyond caricature or a purely polemical engagement. We seek first to understand and to locate the perspective of the other within their theological context. Further, it is important to appreciate that within each of these views there is development. It is essential for us to appreciate that the Roman Catholic doctrine of the Eucharist, or the Lord's Supper, has not been static since the Council of Trent. The Second Vatican Council demonstrated for Catholic Christians the vital connection between the Lord's Supper and the church, for example; and further, there has been an explosion of creative and insightful theological reflection since Vatican II. Thus a volume like this can help readers of other traditions grasp a summary of recent developments and thinking within other views—be they Roman Catholic, Baptist, Reformed, Lutheran or, as noted above, Pentecostal.

Hence, this collection of essays is an exercise in ecumenism: seeking understanding so that the others, even if we differ from them, are a source of insight and learning. And even when, in the end, we differ—as we most assuredly do—what we will inevitably find is that this process strengthens our own understanding of this sacred event in the church's life, the Lord's Supper.

This book will help readers forge their own understanding of the Lord's Supper. What will become apparent is that it is not possible, in the end, to say: I agree with every view and want to adopt bits and pieces of each perspective! Not possible! The reason, quite simply, is that there are substantial differences at the point of first principles: the fundamental reference

---

that Pentecostalism "deserves to be seen as a major Christian tradition alongside the Roman Catholic, Orthodox, and Reformation Protestant traditions," reporting specifically that the number of Pentecostals and charismatics in the world number around 463 million.

points that shape each of these views. Hence, as you read these essays, it is helpful for you to consider each in light of the defining questions that shape one's understanding of the Lord's Supper—three in particular.

The person and work of Christ. We begin with Christology: one's perspective on the meaning of the Lord's Supper is deeply influenced by one's understanding of the nature and ministry of Christ. In particular, we can ask: What is the relationship of the Lord's Supper with the incarnation of Christ Jesus and thus with the whole of the created order? Then also: What is the relationship between the Lord's Supper and the cross—the work of atonement? Further, it is essential to ask: What is the relationship between the Lord's Supper and the resurrection and, indeed, the ascension? This leads to an issue that must also be at the table for dialogue: Is Christ present in this meal? If so, how?

The nature and mission of the church. From Christology we move to ecclesiology. The Lord's Supper is an event of communion and encounter between the risen and ascended Christ and his bride, the church. It is an act anticipating the great event described in the Revelation of John—the "marriage supper of the Lamb." These are the two actors, one might say: Christ on the one hand, and the church on the other. Thus our understanding of this meal will inevitably be shaped not only by our Christology, but also by our theology for the church.

What does it mean to be the church? What is the church? How is the identity and life of the church sustained? And how does this identity find expression in this meal? There certainly are related questions: What is the relationship, if any, between the Lord's Supper and the ordained ministry of the church? And further, Who is welcome at the Table? To whom is it "open"? In particular, one might keep in mind another issue: What is the relationship between baptism and the Lord's Supper? Is baptism a prerequisite for partaking in the Lord's Supper? If so, why? Finally, what is the link, if any, between this sacred event in the life of God's people and their calling into the world? What is the connection or relationship between the Lord's Supper and Christian mission, the church's participation in the in-breaking of God's kingdom?

The nature of the Christian life and the ministry of the Holy Spirit. Then also, we must ask: Of what benefit is the Lord's Supper to the

Christian? What does the Christian and the Christian in community gain from participation in the Lord's Supper? Is the Lord's Supper a means of grace? If so, what is the grace that is known through this practice? Is there benefit for the Christian as an individual, or is the benefit only known "in community," as we participate in the life of the church?

Then also, what is the necessary state or disposition (if any) of the Christian and of the church so that this benefit can be experienced? This includes a pastoral question: How might and should the Christian and the church approach participation in the Lord's Supper? In this context, notable related questions emerge: What is the relationship between the Lord's Supper and the Word, the preached Scriptures? What implications arise from the question of "benefit" that may affect the matter of frequency? How often should the Lord's Supper be celebrated? This naturally means that we attend to the relationship between the Spirit's ministry and the Lord's Supper. It is the Spirit that enables the life of the church and the life of the Christian; and so we ask: What is the relationship between the ministry of the Spirit and the Lord's Supper?

Many of these questions are raised in one of the most extraordinary documents in the history of the church and, without doubt, the most significant publication on the Lord's Supper in the last century: the Faith and Order Commission of the World Council of Churches' document *Baptism, Eucharist and Ministry (BEM)*. Released in 1982, it is the fruit of over fifty years of conversation and debate.[2] Readers of this collection of essays are urged to read *BEM* first, particularly the section on the Eucharist, so that they can properly sense how the stage has been set for this ongoing conversation between representatives of diverse theological traditions.

The *BEM* statement addresses the meaning of the Eucharist, or the Lord's Supper, under five headings: Thanksgiving, Memorial, Invocation of the Spirit, Communion, and Anticipation of the Meal in the Kingdom. It is helpful to read all these contemporary essays or perspectives on the Lord's Supper with the Eucharist section of *BEM* as a guide to the issues and questions that have shaped the conversation about the

---

[2] *Baptism, Eucharist and Ministry*, Faith and Order Paper No. 111 (Geneva: World Council of Churches, 1982) <http://www.oikoumene.org/?id=2638>.

Lord's Supper thus far. We begin to see how different views of the Lord's Supper tend to emphasize one dimension of meaning over another, and all too easily—because one dimension of meaning is especially important to a particular view—another dimension of meaning is neglected. For example, while reading an Anglican commentary on the Lord's Supper, I found the author observing that *BEM* was a good reminder to Anglicans that they had perhaps neglected the emphasis on the Eucharist as a meal of kingdom anticipation and that this perspective needed to be properly brought into the light, and then reflected in words of institution and in the prayers that accompany the celebration of the Lord's Supper. In my own free-church background, *BEM* for me was a revelation of a significant gap in my own tradition: that the emphasis on the invocation of the Spirit and the Spirit's ministry in the Lord's Supper was virtually nonexistent. And this surely is, or at least was, a significant deficiency.

Notable for all Christians is the intentional manner in which *BEM* insists on a trinitarian vision or participation in the Lord's Supper: The Eucharist is a thanksgiving to the Father and in response to the Father's providential goodness, as the "fruits of the earth" are presented to the Father in faith and thanksgiving. The emphasis on the Lord's Supper as memorial recovers the ancient understanding of *anamnēsis,* making present what is recalled and thus providing a clear, or at least clearer, appreciation of the relationship between Christ's original sacrifice and the celebration of that sacrifice at the Lord's Table. The emphasis on the invocation of the Spirit, the epiclesis *(epiklēsis),* reminds Christians that this is ultimately the work of the Spirit in the church.

This benchmark document—*BEM*—has led to a remarkable flurry of studies and publications, evident most notably in the series of "responses" from diverse Christian denominations. It has aptly served to encourage ecumenical studies and clarify some of the continuing points of agreement and diversity of opinion. The authors of this collection certainly hope that the collection of essays you hold in your hand will also further this conversation.

I

THE ROMAN CATHOLIC VIEW

Brother Jeffrey Gros, F.S.C.

It is impossible to understand Catholicism, both Roman (Latin) and Eastern, without realizing three convictions that are central to the hierarchy of revealed truths as the Catholic tradition understands it: (1) the one true church subsists in the Catholic Church, though it is not limited thereto. (2) Christ himself is the primary sacrament, of which the church is a principal mediator through word and sacrament. (3) Catholicism recognizes the real, if imperfect, communion that exists with other Christian churches and therefore is on pilgrimage with them toward that unity for which Christ prayed (Jn 17:21). In this it shares with other Orthodox, Anglican and Protestant churches the goal of the ecumenical movement, as articulated in the World Council of Churches: "to proclaim the ones of the Church of Jesus Christ and to call the churches to the goal of visible unity in one faith, one Eucharistic fellowship, expressed in worship and common life in Christ, in order that the world might believe."[1]

In this essay I will briefly review the Catholic teaching on the Lord's Supper, some of the developments in shared understanding among the

[1] Quoted in preface to *Baptism, Eucharist and Ministry* (Geneva: World Council of Churches, 1982) <www.oikoumene.org/en/resources/documents/wcc-commissions/faith-and-order-commission/i-unity-the-church-and-its-mission/baptism-eucharist-and-ministry-faith-and-order-paper-no-111-the-lima-text/baptism-eucharist-and-ministry.html> (hereafter *BEM*).

churches in the last forty years, and Catholic practice surrounding the celebration of word and sacrament. Because of the centrality of the Eucharist in Catholic ecclesiology, the church's commitment to Eucharistic unity, and its claims to continuity with the faith of the church through the ages, these shared understandings are central to Catholic identity, as this paper should demonstrate. While theology is important, "what makes the Eucharistic action particular and unique is that it is a dynamic, involving event whereby the bonds of time and place are broken and we here and now share in and take part in the very dying and rising of Christ."[2]

Reformed, Lutherans and the free churches, like Catholics, understand quite well that the doctrine of the Lord's Supper is intimately connected to and determined by our Christology. How we understand Christ, his unique mediation and the role of the material world in the incarnation, determines how we understand the church, its visibility, its unity and its ritual life. Finally, our understanding of the eschatological calling of the church is informed and embodied in our understanding of the Supper, as Catholics affirm "by the Eucharistic celebration we already unite ourselves with the heavenly liturgy and anticipate eternal life, when God will be all in all" (CCC §1326).[3]

In fact, we are divided over the Lord's Supper precisely because of our fierce attachment to Christ and our understanding of the relationship of the church in Christ's unique mediatorial role in salvation. The Reformed and free churches fear anything that smacks of idolatry or any mediation that would diminish the sole mediation of Christ. Catholics, Lutherans, Orthodox and some other sacramental traditions would resist any attempt to diminish the concrete, incarnational role Christ uses in church and sacrament, imparting his gracious presence to the people of God. What we say about the Holy Communion discloses to us how we think about the role of the visible church as embodying Christ's mediating presence, and how the incarnation of Christ as truly human and truly divine is related to the community.

In the polemics of the Reformation era, positions hardened and

---

[2] Kevin Irwin, *Models of the Eucharist* (New York: Paulist Press, 2005), p. 308.
[3] Published in *The Catechism of the Catholic Church* (Washington, D.C.: United States Catholic Conference, 1994) <www.usccb.org/catechism/text/> (hereafter CCC).

attempts to understand one another, Catholic and Protestant, Lutheran and Reformed, became increasingly difficult. Modern biblical, patristic, and liturgical scholarship and reform have enabled the churches to deepen their devotion to the one Christ, to appreciate the biblical and historical witness to the Lord's Supper, and to enrich our understanding and styles of celebrating the Lord's Table. The Catholic Church continues to claim that its faith is the "faith of the church through the ages," recognizing a variety of formulations and the necessity of ever developing its doctrinal expressions in new cultures and confronting new debates.

Catholic and Orthodox churches have never completely repudiated one another's understanding of the Lord's Supper and its ministers, though they have been divided at the Table since the Middle Ages. Protestants and Catholics share the Augustinian understanding of sin and grace, of symbol and church, and Anselm's emphasis on the substitutionary atonement as informing our theology of sacrifice. Western theologies of the Supper, including Reformation debates, are more informed by Aristotelian than Platonic resources, which predominate in the East. Eastern liturgy and understanding of sacrifice is more informed by Christ's resurrection and the role of the Holy Spirit, while Christ's saving death and legal categories predominate in the West.

THE CATHOLIC FAITH

Catholic understanding of itself as a church claims an unbroken heritage developed organically and faithfully, with continual reform from apostolic times to the present. Therefore, understanding its teaching on the Lord's Supper will entail looking not only at the biblical tradition as enunciated by Paul (1 Cor 10–11), the Synoptics (Mt 26:26-28; Mk 14:22-26; Lk 22:14-23) and John (6). It will also require a careful exploration of the interpretation of this biblical witness in the heritage of the church, especially as enunciated in the general councils, notably Lateran IV (1215), Trent (1545-1563) and Vatican II (1962-1965).[4] This teaching is conveniently summarized in the 1992 Catechism of the Catholic Church.[5]

---

[4]Norman Tanner, S.J., *Decrees of the Ecumenical Councils*, 2 vols. (Washington, D.C.: Georgetown University Press, 1990), Vatican II, in vol. 2, pp. 817-1113 (hereafter Vatican II).
[5]CCC §§1322-1405.

However, to understand the fullness of Catholic life, it is important also to look at Catholic liturgical life and ritual (CCC §§1345-1361), personal piety of the Catholic people in its worldwide variety (CCC §§1370-1372, 1384-1397, 1402-1405), and the forty years of ecumenical dialogue to which the Catholic Church has been committed (CCC §§1398-1401).[6] Like other Christians, Catholics use the language of thanksgiving, the Eucharist, when speaking of the Lord's Supper in theological terms. In exploring Catholic Eucharistic understanding, a variety of perspectives like cosmic celebration, effective word of God, memorial of the Paschal Mystery, covenant renewal, food for the journey and work of the Holy Spirit—all these are important, as well as terms for Lord's Supper, Eucharist, active presence and sacramental sacrifice (SC[7] in Vatican II; CCC §§1328-1332, 1358-1365). Most popularly Catholics use the term *Mass* from the closing mission-oriented blessing: *Ite, missa est*, "Go, you are sent" (CCC §§1328-1332).

For those unfamiliar with the Catholic tradition in detail, the sixteenth-century contentious issues—the mode of Christ's presence in the sacrament and the relationship of the Lord's Supper to Christ's unique sacrifice—are of most interest. However, to focus on the mode or presence, or to describe the Eucharist solely as sacrifice, obscures its "inexhaustible richness." In the "Decree on the Most Holy Eucharist" (1551), the Council of Trent affirmed that in instituting this sacrament, Christ poured out, as it were, in this sacrament the riches of his divine love for all persons, "causing His wonderful works to be remembered" (cf. Ps 111 [110]:4), and he wanted us when receiving it to celebrate his memory (cf. 1 Cor 11:24) and to proclaim his death until he comes to judge the world (cf. 1 Cor 11:26). His will was that this sacrament be received as the soul's spiritual food (cf. Mt 26:26), which would nourish and strengthen those who live by the life of him who said: "Whoever eats me will live because of me" (Jn 6:57) (Council of Trent, session 13, chap. 2).[8]

---

[6] Most of these dialogues can be found on the Web: <www.prounione.urbe.it/dia-int/i_dialoghi.html> and <www.usccb.org/seia/>.

[7] Decree on the Sacred Liturgy, Sacrosanctum Concilium §47, in Tanner, *Decrees*, pp. 820-43 (hereafter SC) <www.vatican.va/archive/hist_councils/ii_vatican_council/documents/vat-ii_const _19631204_sacrosanctum-concilium_en.html>. See Irwin, *Models*.

[8] In much of this section the work of the Christian Reformed Dialogue with the Catholic Church

Christ's presence. The normal Sunday service in the Catholic Church is the celebration of word and sacrament. Three lessons from the Bible are read, one from the Hebrew Scriptures, one from the New Testament Epistles or Acts, and one from the Gospels. In this proclamation the community focuses on Christ's presence in his revealing Word. Each Sunday also includes the celebration of the sacrament of the Eucharist, where Christ is encountered in the reception of bread and wine, in which his bodily as well as spiritual presence is received.

> At the heart of the Eucharistic celebration are the bread and wine that, by the words of Christ and the invocation of the Holy Spirit, become Christ's Body and Blood. Faithful to the Lord's command the Church continues to do, in his memory and until his glorious return, what he did on the eve of his Passion: "He took bread. . . ." "He took the cup filled with wine. . . ." The signs of bread and wine become, in a way surpassing understanding, the Body and Blood of Christ; they continue also to signify the goodness of creation. Thus in the Offertory we give thanks to the Creator for bread and wine, fruit of the "work of human hands," but above all as "fruit of the earth" and "of the vine"—gifts of the Creator. (CCC §1333)

One not informed by the history of formulations about the Eucharist should be cautious so that the word *bodily* is not misunderstood. When Catholics seek to explain the mystery of Christ's presence in the bread and wine, we generally proceed by way of the *via negativa*. Among the steps taken along that way is the denial of a localized or fleshly presence. Externally, the bread and wine retain their appearance even after consecration. Yet at the same time the whole Christ is sacramentally present in them—the whole Christ, body and blood, soul and divinity. Thus he is indeed "bodily present in the form of bread and wine."

The sacramental encounter with Christ in the community is a mystery, as the Council of Trent affirms and the Catechism reiterates, so that any explanation falls short. In the course of centuries, however, to settle dis-

---

in the United States and Canada is quoted or paraphrased in order to summarize Catholic teaching; see Jeffrey Gros, "Mission and Mystery: Gospel Testimony in Service to the World," in *That the World May Believe: Essays on Mission and Unity in Honour of George Vandervelde*, ed. Michael W. Goheen and Margaret O'Gara (Lanham, Md.: University Press of America, 2006), pp. 155-72.

putes over the meaning of the sacrament, the philosophical wisdom and vocabulary of the day was employed to enhance theological clarity. We should not see any explanations that are given as rationalistic attempts to explain away God's initiative. Instead, we must understand them within the worldview and language system in which they emerged and against the background of the debates they were meant to heal.

The Catholic Church has used the term *transubstantiation* to explain the bodily presence of Christ in the sacrament. Needless to say, most ordinary Catholics do not focus on these theological reflections, but on their personal encounter with Christ in the Mass. The Catholic theologians emphasize the importance of affirming the real presence of Christ and the change of the elements of bread and wine. The doctrine of transubstantiation has been used in order to give a theological articulation to this faith. Although other explanations of this presence would be possible, none has yet been approved by the Catholic Church.

To grasp this explanation, it is important to understand the theological context in which it arose and not to confuse the modern, scientific understanding of "substance" and "change" with the use of the same language in the medieval worldview, with its reliance on the resources of Plato and Aristotle.[9] "Substantial" change was used precisely to avoid any superstitious hint of a physical, chemical or biological change, or the notion that Christ's presence is in space, time, place, quantitatively or qualitatively—all of which are "accidents" in the philosophical systems used in this explanation. The debate as to whether Christ's body is present on the altar/table or in heaven would appear absurd to theologians who understood this explanation.

When critics affirm that they "do not believe in transubstantiation" (or that they do!), it is necessary to ascertain which meaning of "substance" and "accidents" they are affirming or denying. In our scientific ethos, "substance" evokes the periodic chart of elements and translates more readily what Aquinas meant by "accidents" (CCC §§1373-1381).

Today, if philosophical categories are called on to throw light on this mystery, theologians often prefer "relational" categories to "substantial"

---

[9] See Gary Macy, *Treasures from the Storeroom: Medieval Religion and the Eucharist* (Collegeville, Minn.: Liturgical Press, 1998); David Power, *The Sacrifice We Offer: The Tridentine Dogma and Its Reinterpretation* (New York: Crossroad, 1987).

ontology.[10] However, Catholics will tenaciously hold to the faith that Christ is given to us freely by the marvelous initiative of God, by the power of the Holy Spirit. Any hint of a mere human work of memory or reductionistic exclusion of God's objective action in the Supper will be rejected. While the Council of Trent does not require the term *transubstantiation*, it condemns those who would reject its use by Catholics.

Relationship to Christ's once-and-for-all sacrifice. In the teaching of the Catholic Church, the sacrifice of the Mass does not stand in competition with Christ's sacrifice but sacramentally re-presents it. The duplication of the term *sacrifice* in describing both Christ's gift on the cross and the gift of the Mass presents no problem from the Catholic perspective because of a theology of sacramental re-presentation (CCC §§1356-1372).

In the sacrifice of the Lord's Supper, the same victim is indeed offered but in an entirely different *way:* sacramentally. By virtue of this sacramental re-presentation, the Eucharist—far from being "basically nothing but a denial of the one sacrifice" (as the Heidelberg Catechism claims)— renders present the unique and unrepeatable sacrifice of Jesus Christ. At the Last Supper, Christ left the church with "a visible sacrifice (as human nature demands)," which in a bloodless manner "re-presents," makes present, the bloody sacrifice that was once-for-all accomplished on the cross. In this way the "salutary power" of the cross "is applied for the forgiveness of sins" (Trent, session 22, chap. 1). In the "unbloody oblation" of the Eucharist, the "fruits" of the bloody oblation are "received" (Trent, session 22, chap. 2).

Similarly, the *Catechism of the Catholic Church* affirms, "The Eucharist is the memorial of Christ's Passover, the making present and the sacramental offering of his *unique* sacrifice, in the liturgy of the Church which is his Body" (§1362; in §1382 the term used is "perpetuated").

In addition to re-presenting Christ's sacrifice, the Eucharistic sacrifice perpetuates the sacrifice of the cross:

> At the Last Supper, on the night he was betrayed, our Savior instituted the Eucharistic sacrifice of his Body and Blood. This he did in order to perpetuate the sacrifice of the Cross throughout the ages until he should come

---

[10]David Power, "Roman Catholic Theologies of Eucharistic Communion," *Theological Studies* 57, no. 4 (December 1996): 587-610.

again, and so to entrust to his beloved Spouse, the Church, a memorial of his death and resurrection: a sacrament of love, a sign of unity, a bond of charity, a paschal banquet in which Christ is consumed, the mind is filled with grace, and a pledge of future glory is given to us. (SC in Vatican II)[11]

Thus in the Catholic view the Eucharistic sacrifice is not another sacrifice but is the memorial perpetuation of Christ's once-and-for-all sacrifice on the cross.

Hence, when some Protestants conclude that the sacrifice of the Mass detracts from the sufficiency or finality of Christ's sacrifice, that according to the Catholics is unwarranted because it misconstrues the Catholic Lord's Supper as standing in competition with the cross. This caricature is explicitly repudiated by Trent: "By no means, then, does the latter [the unbloody oblation] detract from former [the bloody oblation]" (Trent, session 22, chap. 2). Trent condemns anyone who says that the sacrifice of the Mass "detracts from" Christ's sacrifice on the cross (Trent, session 22, canon 4).

BUILDING COMMUNION

One of the most contentious issues among the churches since the sixteenth century has been the Lord's Supper. Therefore, one of the most dramatic developments in the last century and a half has been the ecumenical reform. This has occurred within churches through their return to the sources, renewal of their forms of worship and the purification of their understanding of the Eucharist through biblical and historical research in the tradition. One of the results of this internal renewal has been the formal ecumenical dialogues, focusing on common sources in revelation and the life of the church through the ages. The ecumenical progress among the churches will not be surveyed here; it is the subject of another section of this book. However, recognizing Catholic developments is essential for us to understand this church's commitments, progress in dialogue and hopes for Eucharistic reconciliation.

Since 1964 the Catholic Church has been fully committed to this ecumenical dialogue. Since the late nineteenth century, biblical and liturgical renewal have set the stage for widening the common ground, first

---

[11] SC, in Tanner, *Decrees*, pp. 820-43; §47 on p. 830.

of understanding and then of agreement with Orthodox and Reformation churches. Because the Lord's Supper is the source and summit of the Christian life, as Catholics understand it, communion at the Lord's Table has been the central expression of the nature and unity of the church, and excommunication of two communities from one another has been the symbol of breaking church unity. We will know that the biblical *koinōnia* is restored when we are able, again, to partake together at the one Table of the Lord. For Catholics, this will entail resolving issues of the apostolic faith, sacramental life and appropriate bonds of communion in the exercise of our common Christian mission in the world.

In this section I will briefly point the reader to three venues in which Catholic reconciliation on the Lord's Supper has developed: (1) World Council discussions, (2) bilateral discussions between pairs of churches, and (3) a German research project on the condemnations of the sixteenth century.

The purpose of ecumenical dialogue is to get behind polemical formulations of the past and reach the core of the faith, expressed in biblical language and terms consistent with the tradition, and not to rehash the polemical debates of another era. Ecumenical research is a search for the truth of Christ, which will be the reconciler of our divided churches, and not a search for compromise or dilution of Christian revelation.

World Council. It is widely recognized that of the three sections of the classical Faith and Order convergence text, *Baptism, Eucharist and Ministry (BEM)*, the Eucharist section is most successful.[12] The 1982 text is the result of over fifty years of dialogue, a century of liturgical and theological return to the sources, and the responses of hundreds of churches, theological faculties and local ecumenical study groups. In the twenty-five years since the publication of the text, it has contributed to rich further study and agreement, a variety of church unions around the world, and renewal in many churches and local communities.

This text is widely known and thoroughly studied and therefore will not be reviewed in detail here. It will suffice to note the Catho-

---

[12] *Baptism, Eucharist and Ministry: Report 1982-1990* (Geneva: World Council of Churches, 1990); Max Thurian, ed., *Churches Respond to BEM: Official Responses to the "Baptism, Eucharist and Ministry" Text*, vols. 1-6 (Geneva: World Council of Churches, 1986-1988); Michael Fahey, *Catholic Perspectives on Baptism, Eucharist and Ministry* (Lanham, Md.: University Press of America, 1986).

lic response as a source for understanding current concerns in the ecumenical conversations. The retrieval of the classical understandings of
anamnēsis has helped to transcend differences over how Christ's once-and-
for-all sacrifice is related to the Lord's Supper (CCC §1354). The theology of the *epiklēsis*, in which Eastern understandings of pneumatology have
softened the Lutheran/Catholic and the Reformed/free church
polarizations of the sixteenth century, has also made an important contribution (CCC §1353).

As George Vandervelde notes, "To discern the ecumenical direction
in which this Vatican document [*BEM* response] points, it is crucial to
examine carefully the issues on which it demurs, and—perhaps even more
importantly—the *manner* in which it demurs."[13] The text only claims to
be a convergence, not an agreed-upon consensus or a basis for restoring
communion at the Lord's Table.

However, the very serious detail of the Catholic response demonstrates
(1) its commitment to the pilgrimage toward full communion at the Lord's
Table, (2) the misunderstandings corrected by the text, and (3) clarification
of areas that will need further work in the next stage of research. So the seriousness of the disagreements demonstrates agreement with and commitment
to the process, and openness to Christ's call to communion at the Table.

In the Vatican response, Catholics ask for a clearer link between the
action of Christ and that of the church in the Supper, a further explication
of the meaning of the memorial *(anamnēsis),* a deepening of the understanding of sacrifice and offering, and a more explicit affirmation of the
change that takes place in the celebration:

> The text in §4 speaks of the bread and wine as a locus for the presence of
> the world at the Eucharist, and as "fruits of the earth," "presented to the
> Father in faith and thanksgiving." But the identity between the gift which
> Jesus Christ makes of his life and the sacramental gesture of the church
> requires that it be made clear that the gifts of bread and wine, the visible
> expression of what is being celebrated here and now, are the sacramental
> signs of Christ's presence.[14]

---

[13] George Vandervelde, "Vatican Ecumenism at the Crossroads? The Vatican Approach to
Differences with *BEM*," *Gregorianum* 69, no. 4 (1988): 691.

[14] Thurian, *Churches Respond*, 6:18.

And in affirming the section on sacrifice, it also raises some issues for further discussion:

> But at several points (§8, commentary 8-9) the notion of intercession is used in a way that could seem insufficient to explain the sacrificial nature of the Eucharist in the Catholic sense. The statement that the Eucharist is the "sacrament of the unique sacrifice of Christ" (§8) refers to the relationship between the historical sacrifice of the cross and the Eucharistic celebration. The link between the historical event of the cross and the present efficacy of that event is the crucified and risen Lord, established as High Priest and "Intercessor."[15]

Catholics recognize a more intimate link between the sacrifice of the Mass and the unrepeatable, bloody sacrifice of Christ on Calvary.

After expressing its appreciation of the affirmations of real presence, the use of *anamnēsis* and *epiklēsis*, the Catholic response to *BEM* goes on to clarify several areas where it considers further work to be necessary:

> The statement about the fact and the mode of Christ's "unique presence," which "does not depend on the faith of the individual," is adequate. But Catholic faith links the sacrificial aspect of the Eucharist to the sacrament of the body and blood more closely than is done in the text. . . . Only in so far as Christ offers himself to the Father as the sacrificial action of the church's liturgy do the elements become sacrament of his self-offering to the communicants. . . . On the other hand, we must note that for Catholic doctrine, the *conversion* of the elements is a matter of faith and is only open to possible new theological explanations as to the "how" of the intrinsic change. The content of the word "transubstantiation" ought to be expressed without ambiguity.[16]

Furthermore, the sacrificial dimension of the Eucharist is affirmed in *BEM* also, but the Catholic response comments that "it does not say unambiguously that the Eucharist is in itself a real sacrifice, the memorial of the sacrifice of Christ on the cross."[17]

Bilateral discussions. The most effective work in resolving old misunderstandings and theological differences among Christians has been bilateral dialogue between the Catholic Church and other churches of

---

[15] Ibid., 6:20.
[16] Ibid., 6:21-22.
[17] Ibid., 6:20.

both East and West. One cannot study the sixteenth century, for example, without taking into account this scholarship of the last forty years.[18]

Among the Western churches the process of agreement has moved more slowly than between Catholic and Orthodox, as one would expect. On such divisive issues as the mode of Christ's real presence in the Supper and how the sacrifice of the cross is related to our celebration of its memorial and the Lord's Table, certain agreements have produced consensus texts from Lutherans,[19] including Lutheran Church–Missouri Synod,[20] and Anglicans.[21] Because for Catholics and Anglicans a resolution on communion in ordained ministry is necessary if communion at the Lord's Table is to be restored, differences over the ordination of women remain to be resolved.[22] Although significant progress has been made on the relationship of ordained ministry, episcopacy and the celebration of the Lord's Supper, this issue is yet to be fully resolved between Lutherans and Catholics.[23]

In conversation with evangelicals and the Reformed churches, issues are even more challenging.[24] However, as the international Reformed Catholic dialogue reports, there are new promising developments.

The background research on the early church's Lord's Supper, the Last Supper, and the Jewish roots of our Eucharistic faith are used to provide a common basis out of which to sort out remaining differences. In this context, historic formulations can be reinterpreted:

For example,

- In the words of institution the emphasis is on the fact of the personal

---

[18] See, for example, Geoffrey Wainwright, *Is the Reformation Over?* [Père Marquette Theology Lecture] (Milwaukee: Marquette University Press, 2000); or Mark Noll and Carolyn Nystrom, *Is the Reformation Over? An Evangelical Assessment of Contemporary Roman Catholicism* (Grand Rapids: Baker Academic, 2005).

[19] See the Lutheran/Roman Catholic Joint Commission text on the Eucharist <www.prounione. urbe.it/dia-int/l-rc/doc/i_l-rc_eucharist.html>.

[20] "The Eucharist" (1968) and "Eucharist and Ministry" (1970), in *Building Unity*, ed. Jeffrey Gros and Joseph Burgess (New York: Paulist Press, 1989), pp. 91-124.

[21] See <www.prounione.urbe.it/dia-int/arcic/doc/i_arcic_final.html> and <www.prounione.urbe.it /dia-int/arcic/doc/i_arcic_classifications.html>.

[22] See <www.prounione.urbe.it/dia-int/arcic/doc/i_arcic_responseva.html>.

[23] See <www.prounione.urbe.it/dia-int/l-rc/doc/i_l-rc_ministry.html> and </www.usccb.org/seia /koinonia.shtml>.

[24] As a sampling of the dialogues, see Daniel S. Mulhall and Jeffrey Gros, eds., *The Ecumenical Christian Dialogues and the Catechism of the Catholic Church* (New York: Paulist Press, 2006), pp. 125-62.

presence of the living Lord in the event of the memorial and fellowship meal, not on the question as to how this real presence (the word "is") comes about and is to be explained.

- When Christ gives the apostles the commission "Do this in remembrance of me!" the word *remembrance* means more than merely a mental act of "recalling."

- The term *body* means the whole person of Jesus, the saving presence of which is experienced in the meal.[25]

At this point the dialogue bases its agreement on a common Chalcedonian Christology and the full trinitarian context of ecclesiology and sacramental theology, shared by the heirs of Calvin and the Catholic Church. Applying this christological confession, the agreement continues:

> The terminology which arose in an earlier polemical context is not adequate for taking account of the extent of common theological understanding which exists in our respective churches. Thus we gratefully acknowledge that both traditions, Reformed and Roman Catholic, hold to the belief in the Real Presence of Christ in the Eucharist; and both hold at least that the Eucharist is, among other things,
>
> - a memorial of the death and resurrection of the Lord;
>
> - a source of loving communion with him in the power of the Spirit (hence the *epiklēsis* in the Liturgy), and
>
> - a source of the eschatological hope for his coming again.[26]

The text goes on to explore common teaching on the mission dimension of the Eucharist.

Condemnations study. A very interesting theological research project was carried out among Reformed, Lutheran and Catholic scholars in the 1980s in Germany to ascertain if the sixteenth-century condemnations are still operative in light of current theological and confessional positions of the three traditions. The resulting agreement on justification and the formal signing of the Joint Declaration of the Doctrine of Justification in 1999 is now an established fact of Christian history and will not be

---

[25] See <www.prounione.urbe.it/dia-int/r-rc/doc/i_r-rc_1-5.html>.
[26] Ibid.

recounted here.[27] However, study of the Eucharist was among the themes treated in this German theological project.

Sacrifice. These studies survey the Reformation confessions and Council of Trent in great detail, indicating the distinctions, differences and condemnations, with the theology that stands behind them. It concludes that both the clear intent of the churches and the modern scholarship do not warrant condemnation of Catholic and Protestant concerns about the uniqueness of the sacrifice of the cross and its relationship to the church's celebration of the Lord's Supper/Eucharist or on the priestly character of the church's participation in this one sacrifice:

> The Reformers bring their criticism to a point in the thesis that the Roman doctrine about the sacrifice of the mass contradicts *the full sufficiency of Christ's sacrifice on the cross, which was once and for all.* The atoning act of Jesus Christ on the cross, accomplished once and for all, requires neither multiple repetition nor any addition or complement. But this acknowledgment of the uniqueness and full sufficiency of the atoning event in Jesus Christ is clearly shared by the Council of Trent, since it defines the sacrifice of the mass as making present *(repraesentatio)* of Jesus Christ's once-for-all sacrifice of himself on the cross.[28]

> It is possible for both sides today to understand the relationship between the sacrifice on the cross, which took place once and for all, and the Eucharistic celebration, as a single yet inwardly differentiated complex.[29]

In looking at the whole study, it is clear how common understandings of justification, the role of good works and the mediatory character of the church are necessary before agreements are possible to resolve the problem of Eucharistic sacrifice.

Presence. The issue of transubstantiation is seen to be complex and requires a historical excursus to provide a common history before a common interpretation of the different formulations can be presented. The German scholars developed a common historical evaluation of Augustine, the medieval debates, and Eastern Eucharistic theological and ecclesiol-

---

[27] See <www.elca.org/ecumenical/ecumenicaldialogue/romancatholic/jddj/declaration.html>.

[28] Karl Lehmann and Wolfhart Pannenberg, eds., *The Condemnations of the Reformation Era: Do They Still Divide?* trans. Margaret Kohl (Minneapolis: Fortress Press, 1990), p. 85.

[29] Ibid., p. 86.

ogy in order to find a common ground for consensus.

The excursus notes that the ninth-century controversies introduced a polarization between sacramental symbol and the truth signified, a polarization neither characteristic of Augustine earlier nor of high scholasticism of the thirteenth century: "And by introducing a cleavage of this kind into the sacramental concept, this viewpoint very soon became a genuine threat to the Eucharist. For the theological positions of the medieval Eucharistic disputes swing between extremes of a heavily materialistic misunderstanding and an equally mistaken spiritualization."[30] The Aristotelian philosophy was drawn on to correct this polarization:

> The metaphysical concept of *substantia* (substance, or essential nature) seemed precisely designed to overcome both a crass "materialism" in the understanding of the Real Presence and a purely intellectualist interpretation of "sign" *(signum),* in this way throwing open once more for a comprehension of the Eucharist the spiritual and personal dimension, the dimension of faith. It is in this context that the concept of "transubstantiation" has to be seen.[31]

The German dialogue reviews some contemporary theological speculation and suggests that a *relational ontology* might be a more fruitful avenue in exploring the question of presence. This section of the study has four conclusions, including the following

> Through their sacramental use, the Eucharistic offerings of bread and wine undergo that change which has from ancient times been termed *conversion* or *mutation* ("transformation" or "change"). The "transformation of essence" which takes place in this feast and its offerings of bread and wine, in the power of the Holy Spirit, through the Word, cannot be revoked. It has an eschatological significance and designates the ultimate essence of this "food for eternal life."[32]

The further work of the German dialogue concludes that Protestant condemnation of Catholic reservation (the saving of remaining consecrated bread and wine) and adoration of the reserved sacrament is

---

[30] Ibid., p. 93.
[31] Ibid., p. 94.
[32] Ibid., p. 101.

obviated by the reforms of Vatican II, in which these devotions are clearly oriented toward the celebration and reception of the sacrament. Adoration is given to Christ, not to the accidents of bread and wine. On differences between Reformed and Catholic devotional practice, and differences of belief in the continuing Real Presence of Christ under the appearances of bread and wine—it has still to be determined whether these issues are church-dividing issues.

For Catholics the celebration of the Lord's Supper and Eucharistic sharing are inextricably linked to the reconciliation and recognition of ordained ministries, so these issues are tied together in such a way that one cannot be resolved without the other. Communion at the Lord's Table implies communion in the Lord's ministry in time and space.

Today we not only have the work of individual pioneering ecumenical scholars and irenic spirits. We also have the results of forty years of research, officially sponsored dialogues, and the internal liturgical reform and theological developments in most of our churches. We even have the 1999/2006 Joint Declaration on the Doctrine of Justification between Methodists,[33] Catholics and the majority of Lutherans, which reverses a process that seemed hopeless in 1541, when Calvin, Contarini, Melanchthon and others broke off the dialogue of their era.

CATHOLIC PRACTICE

One of the most vexing problems among believers is the occasion when we are present at one another's Lord's Supper, and different understandings of the nature of the church, of Christ's presence in the community and the Table, and different pieties leave misunderstandings, especially among those of our people whose ecumenical formation is deficient. Non-Catholics also find Catholic devotional life somewhat alien.

Ecclesial sacramental hospitality. All churches recognize some link of the Lord's Table with the understanding of the nature of Christ's church on earth. All recognize that reception at the Table builds up the body of Christ. Most recognize that the Supper celebrates the communion of Christ's disciples with one another and with him. Some churches empha-

---

[33] See <www.prounione.urbe.it/dia-int/m-rc/doc/i_m-rc_appendix.html>.

size building up the body of Christ and practice open Communion, or sometimes interim Eucharistic fellowship short of full Communion. Other churches emphasize celebrating unity and do not share Communion with those who do not share the same apostolic faith and order, a common sacramental life and membership in the true church as they understand it.

The Catholic Church falls into the latter category, along with Lutheran Church–Missouri Synod, Orthodox, and some other churches and ecclesial communities. However, the Catholic Church also recognizes pastoral occasions when, by exception, Eucharistic sharing is possible because of the centrality of the Lord's Supper in God's saving will for the human community. Times of deathly danger have always been occasions for extraordinary sacramental sharing.

Since the Second Vatican Council (1962-1965), still other instances have recommended themselves. The Orthodox can come freely in cases of need, because of the sacramental faith we share, though the Orthodox do not allow their members to receive in a Catholic liturgy, nor do they usually allow Catholics to commune in their churches. There are exceptions: for example, in Syria and India agreements between church leaders make such sharing possible.

Practice with the Reformation churches is more complex. Many reject the Catholic faith in the presence of Christ in the Eucharist and therefore would not themselves come forward, if they are true to their own Protestant principles. Others, while accepting faith in Christ's Eucharistic presence and demonstrating a clear disposition, are not aware of the ecclesiological implications or the levels of confessional commitment to the church entailed in reception. However, current Catholic practice allows those who ask for Communion to discern with a Catholic minister whether the criteria apply: (1) Catholic faith in the sacrament, (2) authentic spiritual need, (3) absence of a minister of one's own church and (4) proper disposition.[34]

When Catholics read what Luther, Calvin and some Anabaptist polemicists have said about the sacrament, they find it curious that

---

[34] See <www.vatican.va/roman_curia/pontifical_councils/chrstuni/general-docs/rc_pc_chrstuni _doc_19930325_directory_en.html>; also see Catholic Bishops' Conferences of England and Wales, Ireland, and Scotland, *One Bread One Body* (London: Catholic Truth Society, 1998), <www .catholic-ew.org.uk/resource/obob/obob03.htm>.

members of these churches would in good conscience want to approach Christ present in the Eucharist celebrated by the Catholic Church. This challenge to Eucharistic understanding and practice is itself a testimony to the enormous pilgrimage on which the Holy Spirit has taken Christians together in the last half century, even when the impulse to sacramental sharing is not yet informed by a clear understanding of the faith in the church and in Christ's mediating role at the Table. We are called to the journey toward full communion in Christ, even if ecclesial communion at the Lord's Table may not be realized for all of us before we meet our Lord face-to-face, where sacraments and mediation will fall away before the eternal banquet table of glory.

Catholic devotions. The center of Catholic devotional life at its best is the frequent celebration of the Eucharist: hearing the Word proclaimed and reception of Christ present in the bread and wine. Most Catholic parishes will have daily celebration of the Mass for the people of the parish, even when there may be a small attendance.

The principal devotional practice officially promoted by the church, outside of the Mass, is the daily office of psalm prayers and Scripture readings, oriented to the liturgical year and the feasts celebrated at the daily Mass. Unofficially, there are a host of practices that are allowed or encouraged.[35] First among these is the study of the daily Scripture readings in preparation for celebration of word and sacrament. Often preachers will have a parish lectionary group to help him prepare for his weekly homily in the Sunday Mass. Ecumenical prayer groups of ministers may study the weekly readings, shared in the common lectionary used in many Catholic, Anglican and Protestant churches, to deepen their own Eucharistic life for their community and their preaching.

Catholics of both East and West reserve the consecrated bread for communion of the sick. In the West, devotion to Christ present in the consecrated bread has developed in ways unique to the Latin tradition. In the Middle Ages, when few laypeople went to Communion, and then only received the consecrated bread, people participated in

---

[35] Congregation for Divine Worship, *Holy Communion and the Worship of the Eucharist Outside of the Mass* <www.fargodiocese.org/EducationFormation/Evangelization/Eucharist/HolyCommunion AndEucharisticWorshipOutsideOfMass.pdf>.

the Eucharist by attending the celebration and by venerating the consecrated elements preserved in the church building or carried in procession through the streets of the cities. Now with the increased emphasis on biblical devotion, on frequent reception of Communion and on reserving remaining consecrated elements primarily for the sick to commune, these private devotions to the reserved sacrament have become less central, and a different emphasis is recommended.

The church now recommends that, in contemplating Christ's presence before the reserved Communion, the desire for reception, the implications for Communion with Christ in the life of the believer, and prayers and biblical readings of the Mass—all these should be the focus of this devotion. Time alone in the Church in the presence of the Blessed Sacrament is a rich period of contemplating Christ and thanksgiving for his gift in the Communion, which is an integral part of the prayer life of many Catholics. While this private devotion is not an official liturgical prayer of the church, it is a rich part of the Christ-centered heritage of Western Catholic piety.

For Catholics, the celebration of word and sacrament is the source and summit of the Christian life. The worship life of the community is the central mystery in Catholic understanding of the church and the unity of the churches. What differences exist between Catholics and fellow Christians are rooted in the understanding of what Christ demands of the church in its fidelity to his divine revelation.

A Lutheran Response

I am obviously on common ground with Brother Jeffrey Gros, since he too confesses that each legitimate Eucharist involves the occurrence of a miracle at the altar involving the elements of bread and wine. Yet the New Testament "Supper" texts do not function as his starting point, which appears rather to be the documents of Vatican II and the pronouncements of the Roman Catholic teaching office (magisterium) stretching back through Trent to earlier times.

Gros hits the nail on the head when he shows how the fraught term "transubstantiation" actually intends the opposite of what it is usually supposed to mean. This term hails from the lofty discipline of metaphysics, not from the departments of chemistry or physics. Alas, few Christians at the present day (myself included) are schooled to appreciate the subtleties of metaphysics.

I likewise appreciate his emphasis that Rome denies the Lord's "local" presence in the sacrament, but I start to shudder when Gros also repudiates Jesus' "fleshly" presence (Yes and no, Brother! This is real flesh on the altar and in our mouths and hearts, which was born of Mary, hung on the cross, and rose again, albeit present now in a supernatural mode!) and seems prepared to settle for the reduction of "bodily" to "personal" presence. Let us not make the sacramental gift other than what the Lord himself states it to be (although I stoutly agree that, where Jesus' body and blood are, there his human soul and eternal divinity are also).

Even though Lutheran-Roman Catholic dialogue has been briskly under way since the 1960s, conversation between the two sides is still in its preliminary stages. We have arrived at mutual courtesy, but we have not yet fully engaged each other at deeper levels. Should this ever take place, then I look forward to discovering, in dialogue with Gros and his coreligionists, to what extent Rome's insistence that "Eucharistic sacrifice" adds not a whit to the sacrifice on Calvary and the Lutheran admission that the Blessed Sacrament is indeed a "sacrificial banquet"—to what extent these views can facilitate breaking the impasse on the issue of "sacrifice" that has dogged our two sides for nearly five centuries. Should rapprochement occur in this area, then ecumenical goals would be startlingly close to realization.

Our editors asked us to relate our stance on the sacrament of the altar to both Christology and ecclesiology, and under the latter heading Gros has zeroed in on the sensitive issue of ministry, following in the footsteps of the *BEM (Baptism, Eucharist and Ministry)* document of twenty-five years ago. While the leading Lutheran fathers (Luther, Gerhard and Missouri's Walther) all insisted that only an ordained minister (in everyday Lutheran parlance, a pastor) may legitimately celebrate Holy Communion, some Lutherans have, alas, departed from this consensus, allowing for lay celebration under certain circumstances. As I read the New Testament data, our Lord mandated the apostles (no laymen!) to celebrate the rite he founded, and the apostolate flowed into the office of bishop-presbyter, attested in Acts and the Epistles. Orthodox Lutherans insist that the sacramental celebrant must be not only a minister by way of contrast to a layman, but also a clergy*man*, in as much as we can (given the defining deed of Christ in calling only male apostles, along with apostolic teaching and practice) recognize no woman as the legitimate holder of this office.

Here is a point of agreement between Gros and myself—and yet he must disappoint me by being unable to acknowledge my own ministerial credentials as one not properly situated in "apostolic succession," since Lutherans in North America enjoy only presbyteral and not episcopal succession, and Rome alleges that we do not "intend" to transmit the actual office that Christ instituted. Even as, on certain points, I come close to a fellow contributor, the painful reality of Christian division still runs dramatically deep.

A REFORMED RESPONSE

People often assume that the Reformed and the Roman Catholic Eucharistic understandings are worlds apart. Yet in important ways the sacramental theology of John Calvin is truly similar to the Catholic position. There are differences, to be sure, but the common ground makes a sustained conversation between Catholics and Reformed a worthy goal.

Brother Jeffrey Gros rightly identifies some of the issues that divide Catholics and Protestants. These issues include the mode of Christ's presence in the sacrament and how Christ's sacrifice on the cross is related to the sacrifice of the Mass. On these two issues, the Reformed and the Catholics differ in important ways. But Gros then identifies other Catholic affirmations that the Reformed tradition wholeheartedly affirms. These include Christ's love, which is poured out on the worshipers in the sacrament, the nourishment of the Eucharistic feast and the proclamation of the Supper.

Gros's brief but succinct explanation of transubstantiation is quite helpful as a point of comparison with the Reformed position. For Catholics, this concept expresses the sure confidence that Christ is present in the Mass, not in a magical sort of alchemy, nor in the sense of spatial location, but in the reality of the relational presence of Christ. When Gros says, "Catholics will tenaciously hold to the faith that Christ is given to us freely by the marvelous initiative of God, by the power of the Holy Spirit," any Reformed believer steeped in a Calvinian sacramental theology would simply say "Amen." As Reformed theologian David Willis actually said, it is not that transubstantiation is too radical a claim but that it is not radical enough; it does not fully affirm the common, earthy elements of loaf and cup as the means by which we are united to Christ.[36] Reformed sacramental theology, in the line of John Calvin, recognizes the union of Christ and believer in the Supper, through the power of the Holy Spirit.

The most significant break between Catholic and Reformed understandings of the Lord's Supper is over the meaning of Christ's sacrifice. Brother Gros says that the Eucharist is both a re-presenting of Christ's sacrifice and a perpetuation of Christ's sacrifice. Although the Reformed tradition gladly affirms memorial re-presenting of Christ's passion and death in the Supper, it does not affirm the idea of a Eucharistic sacrifice that perpetuates the sacrifice of the cross. The language of Vatican II asserts that Jesus instituted the Supper "in order to perpetuate the sacrifice of the Cross throughout the ages until he should come again." Reformed theology emphasizes not only the once-for-all character of Christ's sacrifice, but also the unrepeatability of that sacrifice.

The clear commitment that the Roman Catholic Church has made to ecumenical and bilateral conversations since Vatican II is a strong and encouraging sign that, although significant differences do exist among Christian communities, the Catholic Church wishes to keep dialogue open with other churches.

---

[36] David E. Willis, *Notes on the Holiness of God* (Grand Rapids: Eerdmans, 2002), p. 93.

A BAPTIST RESPONSE

I found Brother Jeffrey Gros's exposition of Catholic beliefs about the Lord's Supper to be quite enlightening. It is honest and straightforward as well as scholarly and irenic. And it helpfully clears up some of the common misconceptions about the Catholic doctrine of the Eucharist. Anyone familiar with Catholic theology has to wonder whether Gros's interpretations of Catholic doctrine are the same as the magisterium's or whether they are his own interpretations, not necessarily shared by the church's magisterium. I choose to give him the benefit of the doubt and believe that what he says in this essay is, indeed, official Catholic teaching. In that case, I am much relieved.

As a free-church theologian, I still cannot accept the idea of Christ's bodily presence in the elements of bread and wine. However, I now have ammunition against my fundamentalist uncle's claim that Catholics "worship food." (I surely corrected that before I read Gros's essay, but his explanation of the idea of Christ's presence is quite helpful in countering such popular distortions.) The gap between the typical free-church understanding of the Lord's Supper and the Catholic teaching (as presented by Gros) is still wide and deep. But it is not nearly as wide and deep as many Protestants and Catholics believe.

First, if I have understood Gros correctly, it is no part of Catholic teaching that the Eucharist involves a second bloody sacrifice of Christ on the altar. It is a re-presentation of Christ's once-for-all sacrifice, making sacrifice present without repeating it. That is much better than what most Protestants think Catholics believe. It still raises questions about the once-for-allness of Christ's atoning death, but at least a major obstacle to Catholic-Protestant understanding is removed by Gros's exposition.

I turn now to transubstantiation. I appreciate Gros's emphasis on the mystery of Christ's bodily presence, but Protestants will probably always find this mystery too mysterious. And they will find such a mystery unnecessary in that surely the grace of Christ can be experienced and Christ himself personally encountered without any change in the elements.

One aspect of the Lord's Supper that Gros does not adequately discuss is the importance of faith. At least it is important for Protestants. "Without faith it is impossible to please God" (Heb 11:6). Protestants are under the impression that Catholics believe it is possible to receive the grace of God through the sacrament of the Eucharist apart from faith (so long as one is not resisting the grace). This doctrine of *ex opere operato* is probably the most significant stumbling block for Protestants. More than anything else in the Catholic doctrine of the Lord's Supper, it appears to border on injecting magic into the sacrament.

Gros's discussion of the importance of interdenominational dialogue is encouraging. Surely we can only come to understand each other's beliefs by means of direct encounter and open, honest discussion. In the meantime, many free churches invite all believers in Jesus Christ to the Table for the sake of true spiritual unity that transcends intellectual differences of interpretation. Withholding sacramental sharing on the basis of disagreement about the nature of the Lord's Supper seems odd to us. What two people think exactly alike about the act? We are not offended by Catholics' closed Communion, but we find it odd and exclusive. It places intellectual understanding above fellowship among disciples of Jesus Christ.

A PENTECOSTAL RESPONSE

I am fascinated by how differently each author in this compendium approaches the assigned topic. Whereas the Lutheran writer, John Stephenson, devotes a significant portion of his essay to considering christological ramifications of sacramentology, the Roman Catholic writer, Brother Jeffrey Gros, begins and ends with the question of the church's unity. In keeping with the "catholic" view of his theological tradition, Gros connects the celebration of the Eucharist with the question of communion and ecumenism—or lack thereof, because of deep divisions over the Lord's Table. Therefore, beginning by citing the common goal of the ecumenical movement as expressed in the World Council of Churches' landmark document *Baptism, Eucharist and Ministry* sets the pace for the sacramental reflections of this noted ecumenist.

Gros succinctly and pointedly summarizes the dilemma of ecumenism with regard to the Lord's Table: "In fact, we are divided over the Lord's Supper precisely because of our fierce attachment to Christ and our understanding of the relationship of the church in Christ's unique mediatorial role in salvation." The pain of division is deeper the more we all love Christ and want to affirm our oneness with the Lord and the Lord's people.

What also strikes me about Gros's essay is the intentional focus on lived Catholic spirituality rather than merely doctrinal pronouncements (which are not lacking for the church with such a long tradition of theological reflection at the highest academic and ecclesiastical levels). The new

Catechism thus becomes a key source for the presentation of the current postconciliar understanding of the Lord's Supper. As a Protestant theologian, in the mid 1990s I had the memorable experience of spending one full year as resident scholar in a Roman Catholic institute, the Institute for Ecumenical and Cultural Research at the Benedictine St. John's University in Collegeville, Minnesota. Though I was barred from the Eucharistic fellowship—and felt the pain as deeply as did my Catholic hosts—I was also daily blessed by the continuing sacramental and liturgical spirituality. Gros's essay breathes the same air, and for me as a Protestant theologian, this is one of its many invaluable lessons.

Although the author comprehensively and helpfully summarizes and assesses the contemporary sacramental understanding of his church, I was looking for some more discussion of the ways certain contemporary Catholic theologians such as Karl Rahner and Edward Schillebeeckx, among others, have developed a "symbolic" understanding of the sacraments in general and the Eucharist in particular. Those attempts have helped many Catholics, as well as the rest of Christians, to appreciate the basic motifs of older theology, which, as the writer rightly observes, operated with what is now an outdated ontology and worldview. Furthermore, I was also expecting a more intentional discussion of the relation of the Eucharist to the question of the ecclesiality: What makes the church to be church? In Catholic theology and ecclesiology, and similarly in the Eastern Christian tradition, the celebration of the sacrament is not only something the church does, but in a real sense the "Eucharist makes the church." The church is where there is the celebration of the Eucharist under the bishop.

2

THE LUTHERAN VIEW

John R. Stephenson

A century ago George Tyrell fired off a famous salvo against Adolf von Harnack, the prince of liberal Protestant theologians notorious for denying the divinity of Christ and his vicarious atonement and for painting the "historical" Jesus as merely an ordinary man who taught nothing but the fatherhood of God and the brotherhood of man. Tyrell charged Harnack with "looking back through nineteen centuries of Catholic darkness" to find "only the reflection of a Liberal Protestant face, seen at the bottom of a deep well."[1]

Duly mindful that "no one knows the Son except the Father" (Mt 11:27), we should beware of imposing on Jesus our Lord the restraints to which all other men are subject. We may therefore expect his Supper to transcend the terms and conditions placed on all other forms of human hospitality.

Yet old prejudices die hard, with the result that many scholars still stubbornly superimpose their (modernist) preconceptions on the Christology of the New Testament. Already during my high school days, I was taught by a learned follower of Rudolf Bultmann that the early apostolic church in Jerusalem advocated an adoptionist Christology. According to that view, the man Jesus was granted a special relationship with God at

---

[1] George Tyrell, *Christianity at the Crossroads* (London: Darton, Longmans, & Green, 1909), p. 44.

his resurrection (itself considered more an event within the hearts of his disciples than something that actually happened to his dead body).

In the ancient church adoptionism was very much a minority position, and its chief proponent, Paul of Samosata, was almost universally vilified for many centuries after his formal condemnation in A.D. 268. In the early Enlightenment resurgent adoptionism went on the offensive in the Unitarian body that broke off from English Presbyterianism. Three centuries further, Paul of Samosata's adoptionist-unitarian Christology has become commonplace in all major church bodies of Western Christendom. Many theologians accordingly take the view that Jesus' relationship with God differs from ours only in degree, not in kind. Those who embrace this acutely reductionist kind of Christology cannot be expected to understand the rite instituted in the upper room as a real irruption of heaven onto earth.

My high school Scripture teacher admitted that all three Synoptic Gospels advanced beyond the parameters of an adoptionist Christology. All three were, he said, to a greater or less degree incarnationist, but he maintained that Paul and John took this tendency to its furthest extent. Both of them had allegedly plundered the resources of pagan mythology and Gnostic thought to present Jesus (quite inaccurately) as a preexistent divine Being who descended into this-worldly time and space; they painted him as the God-man who spoke mysteries and performed miracles and gave himself as a ransom for many.

Since all contributors to this volume, along with our intended target audience, accept the inspiration of Holy Scripture and hence acknowledge its accuracy and submit to its authority, there is no need here to contest at length the premises and conclusions of the history-of-religions school, as summarized in the foregoing paragraph. But it is eminently worthwhile to reflect that no book or stratum of the New Testament ever follows Paul of Samosata in viewing Jesus of Nazareth as a "mere man *[psilos anthrōpos]*" (hence the heresy of psilanthropism). More to the point, the earliest documents contained in the New Testament (the letters of Paul) enter the field with an unabashedly high Christology. The only Christ whom Paul knows is the preexistent Son of God, who in the fullness of time was born of a woman (Gal 4:4) and took on the likeness of sinful flesh (Rom 8:3).

Paul had to engage in titanic struggles to persuade his Galatian flock of the rightness of his perspective on justification and to vindicate his apostolic authority in the eyes of his skeptical Corinthian converts. Concerning one core conviction, though, Paul was obliged to spill no ink in argument, but could presuppose cheerful unanimity between himself and the scattered Christian communities he addressed. Since he begins his letters with a variant of the power-filled blessing "Grace and peace from God our Father and our Lord Jesus Christ," Paul significantly places the crucified and risen Jesus—with no ifs, buts or maybes—on the "divine" side of the aisle. To put it in a nutshell, "Jesus is Lord" (1 Cor 12:3). Just as he does not confuse the one God with the "many gods" of the ancient Greco-Roman world, so by the same token he puts clear blue water between the "one Lord Jesus Christ" and the "many lords" who tyrannize our fallen existence (see 1 Cor 8:5-6). As is well known, Paul does not conceive the "lordship" of Jesus along the lines of earthly potentates or, say, the various grades of the British aristocracy (all of whom, from dukes at the top to barons at the bottom, used to sit in the pre-Tony Blair House of "Lords"). To the contrary, careful study of the Christ hymn in Philippians (2:6-11) must conclude that Paul's "Lord Jesus" is "the LORD Jesus," the only man who can claim as his own the four-letter Hebrew word, known as the sacred tetragrammaton, which used to be rendered "Jehovah" but now is read as Yahweh (cf. Phil 2:10 with Is 45:23). As Martin Luther put it, "This man is God; this God is man."[2] So neither John in the Fourth Gospel nor the Council of Nicaea in its famous creed propounded a higher Christology than was preached by Paul.

A Lutheran theologian cannot regard these opening reflections on Christology as out of place in an essay devoted to the rite that the old Lutherans usually termed the sacrament of the altar or the Lord's Supper, to which North American Lutherans, under Anglican influence, often refer to as Holy Communion. It is no accident that, in normative documents written in 1530 and 1577, the Lutheran Confessions (known as *The Book of Concord* [= Agreement])[3] take sharp aim at the low Christology

---

[2] *Babylonian Captivity of the Church*, 1520, in *Luther's Works, American Edition* [hereafter cited as AE], 55 vols. (Philadelphia: Fortress Press; St. Louis: Concordia Publishing House, 1955), 36:35.

[3] I will be quoting from *The Book of Concord: The Confessions of the Evangelical Lutheran Church*, ed.

of Paul of Samosata.[4] Moreover, in their chief statement on the topic of Christology, these confessions pointedly take the side of Cyril of Alexandria in his controversy with Nestorius,[5] who understood the manhood of Christ as an entity operating quasi-autonomously from his divine person. Nestorius drove a wedge between the Son of God and the Son of Mary, with the result that he regarded Mary as but the mother of Christ the man. Cyril, by way of contrast, confessed the unity of person of the Word made flesh, the Son of God become the Son of Mary, with the result that Mary is the Theotokos, the Mother of God.

Already in 1519, in the course of contemplation on the Christ hymn of Philippians 2, Luther embraced the pattern of Christology developed in the ancient church by Cyril of Alexandria.[6] In the course of his debate with Zwingli and company on the real presence, Luther entered more deeply into this framework. Lutheranism's second theologian, the major figure of the generation after Luther's death, Martin Chemnitz, penned Lutheranism's major work on Christology, in which Cyril of Alexandria features as the most-quoted church father.[7] Chemnitz, celebrated as the "Second Martin," was the chief author of Lutheranism's principal and thoroughly Cyrillian official statement on Christology, which is found in the eighth article of the Formula of Concord.

Distinctively Lutheran Christology may be summarized as follows: While Jesus will eternally possess the true human body and soul that he assumed in Mary's womb at the Annunciation, we may not straitjacket his unique sacred manhood according to the limits encountered in regular human experience. For one thing, his soul and body subsist in a "personal, or hypostatic, union" with the eternal Son of God. For another,

---

Theodore G. Tappert et al. (Philadelphia: Fortress, 1959), hereafter cited as Tappert. The primacy of "Tappert" is currently challenged by Robert Kolb and Timothy J. Wengert, eds., *The Book of Concord: The Confessions of the Evangelical Lutheran Church* (Minneapolis: Fortress Press, 2000).

[4] See Augsburg Confession, art. 1, "the Samosatenes, old and new"; and Formula of Concord, Solid Declaration, art. 8.16 (Tappert, pp. 28, 594).

[5] Formula of Concord, Solid Declaration, art. 8.15ff. (Tappert, pp. 594ff.) Notice well the strong avowal of Mary's Mother-of-God title (and of her perpetual virginity) in Formula of Concord, Solid Declaration, art. 8.24.

[6] See Tom G. A. Hardt, *On the Sacrament of the Altar,* chap. 3, "The Sacrament Does Not Coincide with the Omnipresence of the Body of Christ."

[7] Martin Chemnitz, *The Two Natures in Christ,* trans. J. A. O. Preus (St. Louis: Concordia Publishing House, 1971), p. 542.

his humanity enjoys real "communion" with his divinity (being as it were a bar of iron in the furnace of Godhead). And, third, divine properties or attributes are communicated to Jesus' human nature, including the "divine majesty," which enables him, as man, to know and have power over all things and to be present as and where he wills. Although believing Reformed, Anglican, evangelical and Pentecostal Christians have no truck with Paul of Samosata and other deniers of the incarnation of the Son of God, they have been, are and will for the foreseeable future remain deeply alienated from the Christology of the Formula of Concord, which Lutheranism shares above all with Eastern Orthodoxy. To my best knowledge, Orthodoxy is the only other portion of Christendom that explicitly concurs in Lutheranism's conviction of our Lord's omnipresence according to his human nature.

Paul, not Luther or any preceding church father, was the first to teach that the "Lord's Supper" (1 Cor 11:20) is the "LORD's Supper" in such a way that the chief Actor in this rite is the glorified Jesus seated at God's right hand, who (albeit hiddenly) confronts his assembled church in holy majesty, making bread to be his sacrificed body and wine to be his sacrificed blood, giving these sacred things to be eaten and drunk for the good of believing, repentant persons, but for the chastisement of the unbelieving and impenitent. As Luther defended this doctrine against Andreas Karlstadt, Ulrich Zwingli and Johannes Oecolampadius in the mid- to late-1520s, he demonstrated (quite convincingly, as far as I am concerned) how Paul's solemn warnings in 1 Corinthians 11:27-32 (which present an apostolic commentary on Christ's words of institution, quoted in 1 Cor 11:23-25) only make sense on the assumption that both Jesus and Paul locate the Lord's "real presence" in the consecrated elements of bread and wine and not merely in the hearts of communicants. The nineteenth-century Lutheran hero of Silesia, Johann Gottfried Scheibel (who was dismissed from his university professorship by a persecuting Reformed king), followed Luther in pointing out that, according to 1 Corinthians 10:16, the body and blood of Christ are received through the acts of eating and drinking, which means that Paul understood the Lord's words in their most obvious sense, to the effect that the consecrated bread *is* his body and the consecrated wine *is* his blood. In other words (and with due apologies for the polemic tone that inescapably accompanies staunch Lutheranism), honest exegesis can understand 1 Corinthians 10:16 only in a Lutheran sense, not in a Reformed sense.

The great debate between Luther and Zwingli, which was carried on for several years through the exchange of major treatises between the two and which culminated at the dramatic colloquy of Marburg in 1529, forms a major episode in church history. My own study of this controversy has convinced me, against the background of the New Testament witness, that—to put it bluntly—Luther was right and Zwingli was wrong. At the same time I must ruefully admit the accuracy of the Anglican bishop Michael Marshall's quip that, while Luther won the battle, Zwingli went on to win the war. After all, with the exception of perhaps one-third of Anglicans, Zwingli has rather much swept the field of world Protestantism. And painful though it is to concede this point, beginning in the seventeenth century, Luther increasingly lost the war for the real presence even in the Communion named after him.

Oddly, although he crafted one of the strongest-ever Lutheran formulations of the real presence in his 1531 Apology of the Augsburg Confession,[8] Philipp Melanchthon was already by this time wavering in his acceptance of this doctrine. Thus in 1534 he traveled to Kassel for negotiations with the "Reformed" party led by Martin Bucer, describing himself in private correspondence as the "emissary for an alien opinion *[nuntius alienae sententiae]*." During Luther's lifetime, Melanchthon privately dissented from Luther's view (shared with the mainline tradition) that the consecration—the celebrant's recitation of Jesus' words of institution—effects the presence of his body and blood on the altar. Melanchthon attacked Luther's liturgical practices as "bread worship," disparaged his reverent consumption of all consecrated elements not distributed at a given celebration, and reduced the presence of the Lord's body and blood to the moment of the reception of the elements, which he associated with the body and blood but did not forthrightly identify with the body and blood. After Luther's death, Melanchthon became

---

[8] Apology of the Augsburg Confession, art. 10.2: "And Vulgarius, who seems to us to be a sensible writer, says distinctly that 'the bread is not merely a figure but is truly changed into flesh'" (Tappert, p. 179).

vitriolic in his public rejection of Luther's doctrine and practice, so that he closed his career as in effect a semi-Calvinist. Those (many) Lutherans who follow Melanchthon rather than Luther in their Eucharistic theology are much closer to low-church Anglicans and the Reformed than they care to suppose.

I thus admit that, concerning the sacrament of the altar, Lutherans are split between the adherents of Luther on the one hand, and of Melanchthon (= the Philippists) on the other, and I lament the numerical superiority of the second of these groupings. Yet I would argue that the "genuine Lutherans" are faithful not only to the testimony of Luther and the Book of Concord, but also—and this is the decisive factor—that Luther's position accords (1) with the words of Christ and Paul, and (2) with the almost unanimous witness of the ancient church.

In all likelihood the first words of the earthly Jesus to be written down in New Testament Scripture, the words of institution as recorded by Paul and the Synoptic Evangelists, are in fact our first line of defense against a low, adoptionist Christology. The Jesus who so dramatically injected novel and unheard-of words and gestures into the last Passover that he celebrated within the circle of his disciples manifestly thinks of himself as the very opposite of an "ordinary man [*psilos anthrōpos*]." For one thing, Jesus views his coming death (which on the Jewish reckoning of time occurs on the same day as the institution of the Eucharist) as an atoning sacrifice. For another, as he commands his apostles (and hence all future apostolic ministers) to continue the celebration of this rite, he clearly envisages the future formation of his church. It is all too easy to overlook the further fact that the speaker of these words also considers himself to be God. No pious Jew would ever drink blood, much less command other people to drink his own blood. Only the God who once forbade the drinking of blood may dispense with this command. Thus the Lord who bids his apostles (and all future communicants at his altar) to drink his blood must be either God in the flesh or a blasphemer. The words of institution themselves demonstrate that one greater than Solomon and the temple he built is here (Mt 12:42, 6), one whose "I" may edit the old law (Mt 5:21-48) and institute a supernaturally efficacious liturgical rite to be observed till the end of time.

In recent ecumenically oriented theology (sometimes even in works by Roman Catholic authors!), the argument has been made that with the words "This is my body," Jesus meant to say, "This is I." In other words, it is contended that Christ meant to teach merely his *personal* presence in the Blessed Sacrament, not his *bodily* presence. Many ecumenists (of all major Western confessions and denominations) consider that common acknowledgment of the Lord's *personal* presence in the Supper should permit us to bypass former bitter disputes over his alleged *bodily* presence so that all Christians may henceforth share a common Eucharistic table in fulfillment of Jesus' prayer in John 17.

While confessing (with Luther) the *personal* presence of the undivided God-man Jesus Christ in the celebration of Holy Communion, I stress that his *real* presence in the Blessed Sacrament is not to be understood as the opposite of some supposed *unreal, fictitious* presence, but as an abbreviation for his *corporeal* presence. And I argue with Luther that this is the doctrine not only of Paul but also of the earthly (and heavenly) Jesus himself. The history-of-religions school admitted that Paul understood the Lord's Supper in this way but dismissed his doctrine as an intrusion of pagan-cum-Gnostic thought into early Christian circles. This route cannot consistently be taken by evangelicals, who operate with a high view of Scripture, and whom I therefore invite to reconsider the historic Reformed position.

The major stumbling block in the way of the ecumenically convenient reduction of the real to the personal presence is found in the terminology deliberately chosen by our Lord in the upper room as he ritually preenacted the greater Passover accomplished on his cross (Lk 9:31). Jesus used the language of the Old Testament sacrificial cultus as he labeled bread his "flesh" and wine his "blood" (cf. Deut 12:27). If he had wanted to teach his merely personal presence in future celebrations of Holy Communion, with the elements functioning only in a symbolic capacity, he could easily have done so, employing for the purpose the terminology he used in Matthew 18:20 and 28:20: "As you eat and drink parable-style bread and wine in my memory, I shall be in your midst." Curiously, the Lord decided to speak otherwise, in the terminology found in Deuteronomy 12:27, which can so easily be taken in the sense unanimously understood by Roman Catholics, Orthodox and Lutherans.

Hermann Sasse, a twentieth-century Lutheran who belonged firmly on the Luther side of the aisle as far as the real presence was concerned, was wont to point out that, whereas Christ often followed up his seemingly opaque parables with a clear explanation, he forbore to do so in the case of the sacramental words that he spoke at the Last Supper. The reason for this omission is that he intended and intends these words to be taken in their fullest sense, not their barest sense. Luther urged that, had Jesus willed to found a memorial supper featuring symbols of his (absent) body and blood, he would have been well advised to retain the old Passover meal, for the slaughtered lamb was a much more apt symbol of his sacrificed body and blood than are the inanimate elements of bread and wine.[9] As I listen to the words once spoken in the upper room that Christ continues to speak through his ordained servants at the altar, I can only concur with the steely riposte of the novelist Flannery O'Connor to the "progressive" post-Vatican-II sacramental musings of her fellow novelist Mary McCarthy. Having earlier (eccentrically!) considered the consecrated host to be the Holy Ghost in person, as the "most portable person of the Trinity," McCarthy now deemed the host "a symbol, and a pretty good one." "I [Flannery] then said, in a very shaky voice, 'Well, if it's a symbol, to hell with it.'"[10]

A symbolic understanding of the elements would have proved helpful to the fathers of the second-century church as they faced the charge that, for their privately conducted Eucharists, the Christians committed ritual murder for the "cannibalism" involved in eating a body and drinking blood. Remarkably, neither Ignatius nor Justin nor Irenaeus took Mary McCarthy's path of least resistance, but instead, to quote only Ignatius, confessed that "the Eucharist is the self-same body of our Saviour Jesus Christ which suffered for our sins and which the Father in his goodness afterwards raised up again."[11] In 1532 Luther applied the Vincentian Canon (orthodoxy = "what has been believed everywhere, always, and by everybody") to

[9] AE 37:264 (*Confession Concerning Christ's Supper*, 1528).

[10] Quoted in James T. O'Connor, *The Hidden Manna: A Theology of the Eucharist* (San Francisco: Ignatius Press, 1988), p. 95.

[11] Ignatius of Antioch, *Letter to the Smyrnaeans*, 7, in *Early Christian Writings: The Apostolic Fathers*, ed. Andrew Louth, trans. Maxwell Stanforth (New York: Penguin Books, 1987), p. 102.

the issue of the Lord's sacramental presence, observing how "it is a peril-ous and dreadful thing to hear or believe anything against the unanimous testimony, belief, and doctrine of the entire holy Christian church."[12]

For Luther—and the Book of Concord[13]—the sacramental presence is realized in the divine service at the consecration of the elements, which occurs through the celebrant's pronouncing the words of institution over the elements "in Christ's person and name."[14]

> We speak the divine, almighty, heavenly, and holy words which Christ him-self spoke at the supper with his holy lips and commanded us to speak.[15]

> For as soon as Christ says, "This is my body," his body is present through the Word and the power of the Holy Spirit. If the Word is not there, it is mere bread; but as soon as the words are added they bring with them that of which they speak.[16]

> Here too, if I were to say over all the bread there is, "This is the body of Christ," nothing would happen, but when we follow his institution and command in the Supper and say, "This is my body," then it is his body, not because of our speaking or our declarative word, but because of his com-mand in which he has told us so to speak and to do and has attached his own command and deed to our speaking.[17]

The statements of Luther and the Confessions quoted in the forego-ing paragraphs align orthodox Lutherans with the Roman and Ortho-dox churches with respect to the Blessed Sacrament and, on this point at least, erect an insuperable wall of separation between orthodox Lutheran-ism and the wide world of Protestantism.[18] Conversely, Melanchthon's

---

[12] Quoted by John R. Stephenson, *The Lord's Supper*, vol. 12 of *Confessional Lutheran Dogmatics* (St. Louis: Luther Academy/Logia, 2003), p. 237.

[13] Formula of Concord, Solid Declaration, art. 7.73-87 (Tappert, pp. 583-85).

[14] "But when he said, 'Do this,' by his own command and bidding he directed us to speak these words in his person and name: 'This is my body'"; AE 37:187 (Martin Luther, *Confession Concerning Christ's Supper*, 1528).

[15] AE 40:212 (Luther, *Against the Heavenly Prophets*, 1525).

[16] AE 36:341 (Luther, *The Sacrament—Against the Fanatics*, 1526).

[17] AE 37:184 (Luther, *Confession Concerning Christ's Supper*, 1528).

[18] This statement made by Luther less than two years before his death (and quoted with approval by the Formula of Concord, Solid Declaration, art. 7.33; Tappert, p. 575) proves that the Luther-ans who have entered into fellowship arrangements with Anglicans have at least fudged their

disavowal of the efficacious consecration caused Lutherans of his ilk to drift ever closer to Reformed understandings of the sacramental presence, facilitating the current state of affairs in which perhaps a majority of Lutherans worldwide enjoy Communion fellowship with most of Reformed Christendom.

It would be inaccurate to suppose that Luther's confession of the real presence was only "firmed up" from the outset of his impassioned debate with Karlstadt, Zwingli and Oecolampadius. Some years before the outbreak of this Protestantism-dividing controversy, Luther had contended that his own way of expressing the Eucharistic mystery confessed not a whit less "real presence" than is conveyed through Rome's officially promulgated theory of transubstantiation.[19] Predictably, Melanchthon came to think otherwise, joining with Calvin in the charge that transubstantiation is a major area where Rome went astray in its understanding of the Eucharist. Conversely, Luther always regarded the debate over transubstantiation as a relatively minor issue. In theological treatises he would argue against the dogmatization of an Aristotelian paradigm, but significantly refrained from attacking transubstantiation in homilies before laypeople (for they might have misunderstood him to be denying the real presence itself, should he have done so). The sorest point of Luther's (and orthodox Lutheranism's) confession, from the perspective of Reformed Christendom, is crisply manifested in this remark: "Sooner than have mere wine with the fanatics [the Reformed], I would agree with the pope that there is only blood."[20]

As might be expected, the Reformed threw at Luther and the orthodox Lutherans many of the same charges that they hurled at the church of Rome. For the record, let it be recorded that one of these simply did not and does not stick. The Reformed leveled the accusation that both Rome

confession, while the Lutherans who have established intercommunion with the Reformed have abandoned it. "For they do not want to believe that the Lord's bread in the Supper is his true, natural body which the godless person or Judas receives orally just as well as St. Peter and all the saints. Whoever (I say) does want to believe that, let him not trouble me with letters, writings, or words and let him not expect to have fellowship with me. This is final"; AE 38:304 (Luther, *Brief Confession Concerning the Holy Sacrament*, 1544).

[19] See AE 36:29 (Luther, *Babylonian Captivity of the Church*, 1520).

[20] AE 37:317 (Luther, *Confession Concerning Christ's Supper*, 1528).

and Luther taught a "local" presence of Christ's body and blood in the Blessed Sacrament. Not so, for both Thomas Aquinas and Luther insisted that the Lord's body and blood are not present in the same way as the elements themselves, occupying space and bounded by it. Rather, the body and blood are present supernaturally and in such a way that each tiniest portion of consecrated bread and wine is the Lord's whole body and whole blood.[21] "Each person receives it [the body] whole."[22] Remarkable identity exists on this point between Rome and Luther's Wittenberg, so that it comes as no surprise that a famous Lutheran Eucharistic hymn ("Soul, Adorn Yourself with Gladness" [Johann Franck]) knowingly echoes words of Thomas Aquinas, nor does it appear odd that the Missouri Synod's latest (2006) hymnal contains Thomas's two famous Eucharistic hymns, with the result that some North American Lutherans will shortly be singing: / "Word made flesh, the bread He taketh, / By His word His flesh to be; / Wine His sacred blood He maketh, / Though the senses fail to see; Faith alone the true heart waketh / To behold the mystery."[23]

The different ways in which Lutherans and Roman Catholics articulate the real presence are in themselves not necessarily church-divisive. Lutheran "sacramental union"—according to which, at the consecration, the elements become "flesh-bread" and "blood-wine"[24]—could conceivably coexist with Roman transubstantiation, but this state of affairs will not come about until Lutherans and Roman Catholics agree concerning the sacrificial dimension of the Blessed Sacrament. Concord can swiftly be established on two points, but for the foreseeable future the two sides will remain at loggerheads on a third point. First, Jesus commanded the apostles to give thanks at the celebration of the Holy Supper, so that

---

[21] AE 37:222-23; quoted in Formula of Concord, Solid Declaration, art. 7.98-102 (Tappert, pp. 586ff.). See also AE 38:292-93 (Luther, *Brief Confession Concerning the Holy Sacrament,* 1544). For reflection on Lutheranism's teaching concerning the three ways in which Christ exercises bodily presence, see Stephenson, *Lord's Supper,* pp. 247-58. Note well that we understand the real presence as falling within the "definitive mode" of presence, *not* within the "repletive mode" according to which our Lord is omnipresent according to his humanity. Much confusion exists on this point, even among Lutherans.

[22] AE 38:293.

[23] *Lutheran Service Book: Prepared by the Commission on Worship of the Lutheran Church–Missouri Synod* (St Louis: Concordia Publishing House, 2006), #630, 4 (hereafter *LSB*).

[24] AE 37:303 (Luther, *Confession Concerning Christ's Supper,* 1527).

this rite is indeed the Holy Eucharist, the church's offering of thanks and praise to the Father through the Son in the Holy Spirit.[25] Since the "Eucharistic" dimension of Holy Communion is sometimes downplayed in Lutheran liturgy and practice, other Christians could help us recover a fuller understanding and observance of this aspect of Christ's institution.[26] Second, the Blessed Sacrament is a sacrificial banquet, in which our Lord gives into communicants' mouths the actual flesh and blood once offered for them.[27] But, third, to the extent that Roman Catholics teach that the celebrant actively offers the really-present body and blood to the Father for the living and the dead, Lutherans react in horror that "synergism" has swamped what we call the "divine monergism." That is to say, man is now cooperating toward his own justification, rather than simply passively receiving the fruits of the work uniquely and solely accomplished by the God-man.[28]

In his Large Catechism of 1529, which is included in *The Book of Concord,* Luther crisply sums up the benefits of devout Communion under three headings. In first place, the really present body and blood vouchsafe renewal of forgiveness and cleansing to the believing, penitent communicant. "In other words, we go to the sacrament because we receive there a great treasure [the Lord's body and blood] through and in which we obtain the forgiveness of sins."[29] Second, the sacramental gift is the supernatural manna that sustains the new Israel in its pilgrim journey through the wilderness of this fallen life. "Therefore, it is appropriately called the food of the soul since it nourishes and sustains the new man. While it is true that through Baptism we are first born anew, our human flesh and blood have not lost their old skin. There are so many hindrances and temptations of the devil and the world that we often grow weary and faint, at times even stumble. The Lord's Supper is given as a daily food and sustenance so that our faith may refresh and strengthen itself and

---

[25] See Stephenson, *Lord's Supper,* pp. 116-19.

[26] This process might begin through our contemplation of the appropriate section of the *BEM* (Lima) document: *Baptism, Eucharist and Ministry,* Faith and Order Paper 111 (Geneva: World Council of Churches, 1982), pp. 10-11 (Eucharist, §2.A).

[27] Stephenson, *Lord's Supper,* pp. 111-15.

[28] Ibid., pp. 119-26.

[29] Large Catechism, art. 5.22; Tappert, p. 449. See Stephenson, *Lord's Supper,* pp. 193-98.

not weaken in the struggle but grow continually stronger. For the new life should be one that continually develops and progresses."[30] Third, and in keeping with the testimony of John 6, the Lord's body and blood are Ignatius's "medicine of immortality, the remedy against our having to die," the pledge of future bodily glory, "a pure, wholesome, soothing medicine which aids and quickens us in both soul and body. For where the soul is healed, the body has benefited also."[31] In his major Eucharistic treatise of 1527, Martin Luther put his scriptural, Cyrillian Christology to good use as he responded to Zwingli's charge that, even if Jesus were to give us his body to eat, it could, as a physical thing, do us no good. "God is in this flesh. It is God's flesh, the Spirit's flesh. It is in God and God is in it. Therefore it lives and gives life to all who eat it, both to their bodies and to their souls."[32] "The mouth, the throat, the body, which eats Christ's body, will also have its benefit in that it will live forever and arise on the Last Day to eternal salvation. This is the secret power and benefit which flows from the body of Christ in the Supper into our body, for it must be useful and cannot be present in vain. Therefore it must bestow life and salvation upon our bodies, as is its nature."[33]

As a "sacrificial banquet,"[34] the Lord's Supper obviously belongs in a different ballpark from the potluck suppers held in church basements, to which all and sundry are heartily invited. In ancient Israel only the priests were permitted to eat the "most holy things" offered on the altar, while the laity had to content themselves with partaking of the "holy" peace offerings. Through the rite instituted in the upper room, Christ would have all his people, both clergy and laity, partake with the mouth of the "most holy things" that are his true body and blood. But in order to be eligible for Holy Communion, a person must first of all be baptized, otherwise he or she has not been born again (or from above) by water and the Spirit (Jn 3:5). Second, communicants must be properly instructed in Christian

---

[30] Large Catechism, art. 5.23-25; Tappert, p. 449. See Stephenson, *Lord's Supper,* pp. 198-200.

[31] Large Catechism, art. 5.68; Tappert, p. 454. See Stephenson, *Lord's Supper,* pp. 200-204.

[32] AE 37:124-25 (Luther, *That These Words,* 1527).

[33] AE 37:134 (Luther, *That These Words,* 1527). These references could easily be multiplied from the writings of Luther and the classical Lutheran theologians.

[34] See John W. Kleinig, "The Lord's Supper as a Sacrificial Banquet," *Logia* 12, no. 1 (Epiphany 2003): 11-16.

doctrine in general and in the doctrine concerning the sacrament of the altar in particular (so while orthodox Lutherans may be open to "early Communion," few of us are keen on "infant Communion"). How can infants be expected to "discern the Lord's body" (1 Cor 11:29), which Lutheran exegesis understands as a reference to his historic, sacramental body, not to the church as his mystical body? Third, communicants are to "examine themselves" ahead of sacramental participation, so that they approach the altar with repentant hearts (1 Cor 11:28). Lutheran pastoral wisdom heartily commends private, sacramental confession and absolution by way of preparation for Communion, especially in cases where grievous sin has been committed. Happily, the benefits of private confession are currently being rediscovered among Lutherans in North America.[35]

Yet the Lord's Supper is most emphatically not a means of grace in which the Lord deals with his sheep individual by individual, but rather a setting in which he meets us as an assembly, a collective, a corporate body. Historic Lutheranism has therefore practiced "closed Communion," restricting access to its altars to those who share its confession. Lutheran pastoral practice has always acknowledged exceptional cases where Holy Communion may be given to baptized Christians of another confession who willingly profess the core of Lutheran Eucharistic doctrine, but orthodox Lutherans remain unable to offer "Eucharistic hospitality" as a matter of course. My colleague and former seminary president Jonathan Grothe has often remarked that our practice of closed Communion, which is so offensive to modern sensibilities, finds firm ground in 1 Corinthians 11:26, where not a singular but a plural "you" celebrate the Eucharist: the various confessions are not yet at one in their proclamation of the Lord's death!

Pope Benedict XVI yearns for the establishment of visible Christian unity that would render intercommunion a rightful option. In his recent exhortation *Sacramentum caritatis* he expresses the position historically embraced by the Missouri Synod, as can be seen if we replace "Catholic" with "Lutheran" in the following extract:

The respect we owe to the sacrament of Christ's Body and Blood pre-

---

[35] See *LSB*, #616.

vents us from making it a mere "means" to be used indiscriminately in order to attain that unity. The Eucharist in fact not only manifests our personal communion with Jesus Christ, but also implies full *communio* with the Church. This is the reason why, sadly albeit not without hope, we ask Christians who are not Catholic [Lutheran] to understand and respect our conviction, which is grounded in the Bible and Tradition. We hold that Eucharistic communion and ecclesial communion are so linked as to make it generally impossible for non-Catholic [non-Lutheran] Christians to receive the former without enjoying the latter. (§56)

Orthodox Lutherans agree with Joseph Ratzinger that Eucharistic fellowship is church fellowship, and vice versa, a truth that individualistic modern Christians, insecurely grounded in Scripture and tradition, find a bitter pill to swallow.

A quarter century has now passed since the issuance of the World Council of Churches' *Baptism, Eucharist and Ministry* [*BEM*, or *Lima Document*] in 1982. William H. Lazareth, a prominent U.S. Lutheran theologian, was a major author of the *BEM* proposal that aimed to facilitate a maximum amount of "Eucharistic hospitality" for the benefit of individuals and also to foster an increasing volume of intercommunion between hitherto separated church bodies. Though Lazareth saw to it that *BEM* made welcome statements of substance in the three controverted areas with which it deals, he could not have been unaware that Luther himself and the orthodox Lutheran tradition would have found the hazy language and broad parameters of section 13 of the part on the Eucharist guilty of failing to confess in clear terms the "one thing necessary" concerning the Blessed Sacrament.[36] Yet most North American Lutherans who are obliged in good conscience to reject *BEM*'s offer can be faulted for nurturing next to no yearning for

---

[36] *BEM*, §12. Non-Lutherans should be aware of Lutheranism's bewildering internal complexities. For example, the square off between the great majority that forms part of the Lutheran World Federation (LWF) and the tiny minority that belongs to the International Lutheran Council (ILC) is not a straightforward left-right divide. As global leadership shifts to the Third World, Bishop Obare of Kenya (whose church belongs to the LWF) is emerging as perhaps the major spokesman for orthodox Lutheranism worldwide, while there is minority support within the ILC for practices such as women's ordination. Moreover, having had friendly correspondence with Bishop Lazareth a decade ago, I have a sense that this member of the Evangelical Lutheran Church of America's House of Bishops would be sympathetic with the general drift of this essay, parting company from me chiefly in advocacy of a much greater measure of "Eucharistic fellowship" and probably in openness to intercommunion with Anglicans.

Christian reunion and for venturing hardly any participation in ecumenical activity. Oddly, while their sister churches in Germany and Australia enjoy pivotal ecumenical involvement in their respective countries, there is currently no explicit ecumenical component in the public life of the Lutheran Church–Missouri Synod and Lutheran Church Canada.

Lutheranism has its own distinctive liturgical heritage, which I cherish. With closest affinities to Anglicanism among other major confessions, the Lutheran liturgical tradition has involved a reshaping of the historic Western development in worship according to the doctrine of the Wittenberg Reformation. In my view, the most appropriate liturgical embodiment of the position I have endeavored to set forth in this essay is found in a reverent celebration of the rite found in the Missouri Synod's *Lutheran Hymnal* of 1941, the service known among Missourians simply as "Page Fifteen." In the last generation, since the issuance of *Lutheran Worship* in 1982, the old Page Fifteen (which in slightly modified form is featured as Divine Service One in *Lutheran Worship*) has been eclipsed by the 1960s-feeling Divine Service Two. Yet the old Page Fifteen has demonstrated amazing resilience, now appearing in almost unchanged form (most "Thous" have become "Yous") as Divine Service Three in *Lutheran Service Book*. Many congregations seem to be gravitating once more to this rite, which is deeply inscribed in the subconsiousness of the Missouri Synod. A traditionalist Anglican would feel at home at this service, and a Roman Catholic would know what was going on.

On Palm Sunday 2004, along with a group of fellow Lutheran seminary professors from around the world, I took part in a German-language Eucharist celebrated in Erfurt, the city where Luther once became a monk. Located as it is in the former East Germany, the interior of the church building was in a state of disrepair, and worshipers in the large stone church were obliged to wear overcoats to ward off the lingering winter cold. But the assembly was united in devotion before the large crucifix that hung over the altar, and the celebration of a German version of Page Fifteen turned out to be one of the most reverent and beautiful celebrations I have ever participated in. The congregation fell to its knees at the Sanctus ("Holy, holy, holy"), as did the celebrant when, following blessed Martin Luther's example, he genuflected before the Lord's body and blood at their consecration on the altar. Anyone wanting to know what makes Lutheran Eucharistic doctrine tick should not only read appropriate books and articles, but also visit such a sacramental celebration, which devout participants understand as a real irruption of heaven onto earth. One of Luther's best one-liners on the sacrament of the altar states that the Lord instituted this venerable sacrament "in order to be bodily as close to us right now as he was to his disciples back then."[37] With Luther, and with all my coreligionists who share his confession, what can I say but that "I love it from the heart, this dear, blessed Supper of my Lord Jesus Christ, in which he bodily gives into my bodily mouth His body and blood to eat and drink with these superabundantly sweet and amiable words, 'Given for you, shed for you. . . .'"[38] Blessed be Jesus Christ, true God and true Man, in the most holy sacrament of the altar!

---

[37] Cf. AE 37:94, which offers a less-than-satisfactory translation of the German original found in Weimar Edition 23:193, 6-10.

[38] My own rendering of the German original translated in AE 38:227 (*Luther's Letter Concerning His Book on the Private Mass*, 1534).

A Roman Catholic Response

A word of appreciation to John Stephenson for emphasizing the christological character of our Eucharistic faith, outlining the ecclesiological dimension of Eucharistic participation, and reminding us of the ecumenical contribution of the Lutheran Church–Missouri Synod.

Christians in the sixteenth century, and Baptists and Wesleyans and Pentecostals thereafter, separated from one another over their vehement commitment to Christ at the center of their Christian faith. They differed on their interpretations of the Lord's Supper because of the fierce adherences to Chalcedonian Christology as they understood it, save for a few Anabaptist groups. It is essential to understand that shared christological faith is at the roots of our divisions, and that only by a high christological approach to theological dialogue toward unity will such divisions be healed, contrary to the author's caricature of these theological discussions.

Catholics, as well as Lutherans, need to be formed to understand that "the different ways in which Lutherans and Roman Catholics articulate the real presence are in themselves not necessarily church-divisive," and that Luther's objections to scholastic formulations were less to content than to the danger of rationalizing the faith.

The most painful element in our division is our inability to share Eucharistic Communion. Stephenson rightly outlines the intimate link between celebrating the Lord's Supper and ecclesial fellowship, a position shared by most Christians yet also misunderstood by most Christians, including those in churches who share this confessional position. We do not decline Communion out of lack of respect, or out of denial of Christ's saving presence in the other communities. No one is worthy of the great gift of Christ in the Supper. We do not do so because of obsolete disciplinary norms. Rather, together we try to respect the Pauline admonition about unity at the Table.

Other Christians are grateful for the strong confessional conviction the Lutheran Church–Missouri Synod brings to its ecumenical witness, even though a minority. Missouri theologians were full members of the U.S. dialogue with the Catholic Church through the first nine rounds, and they have had official representation in the tenth and the present eleventh rounds. They have contributed to the *BEM* document *(Baptism, Eucharist and Ministry)*, commented on by Stephenson, and the church has made an official response to the text. Unlike his characterization, *BEM* does not claim to solve Eucharistic divisions, but only to contribute a certain level of convergence. One must look to the bilateral dialogues for a higher level of consensus.

Before claiming that agreement between Catholics and Lutherans on sacrifice is impossible, the author would do well to analyze the U.S. Lutheran-Roman Catholic statement, to which Missouri theologians made important contributions (www.usccb.org/seia/luthrc_eucharist_1968.shtml).

Though Stephenson is right to challenge members of his own church to greater ecumenical commitment, we recognize that such conversion to Christ's prayer for the church's unity is equally a challenge for members of all our churches, no matter how ecumenically committed may be their official positions.

A Reformed Response

The fiery polemics of the Marburg Colloquy in 1529, when Luther and Zwingli went head-to-head over the real presence of Christ in the Lord's Supper, have tended to define the character of Reformed and Lutheran dialogue ever since. Although John Stephenson is convinced that orthodox Lutheranism is in strong continuity with Jesus, Scripture and early Christian tradition, he recognizes that the stream of Zwingli went on to "win the war" on the question of Christ's real presence in the Supper. As a Reformed Christian with deep roots in Calvin's sacramental theology, I can lament this perhaps as much as Stephenson. Yet my desire is to retrieve a full, biblical Lord's Supper understanding along the lines of sacramental theology, not along the lines of Luther and the Book of Concord.

Stephenson reports a profound experience he had of the Eucharist in the former East Germany some years ago. He explains how deeply moving it was to attend such a worship service, where "devout participants" understood the sacrament "as a real irruption of heaven onto earth." I appreciate his telling this story because I think that worship exhibits the fruitfulness of biblically rooted theology.

The Reformed tradition, too, forms worshiping people who are convinced that the Lord's Supper is an "irruption of heaven onto earth." An interesting clarification is that the Reformed tradition understands the believer to be taken up, by the power of the Holy Spirit, into heaven, to be united with Jesus Christ. The motif of "sacramental ascent" that is characteristic of Calvin is consistent with a Reformed understanding of the resurrected and ascended Christ. The perfected human nature of the resurrected Christ is such that Christ's bodily presence is not everywhere, not "ubiquitous." So Calvin uses a range of images to express the quality of the unity between Christ and believer. One image is ascent: the believer "ascends" to where Christ is in heaven, thus to be united with him by the Spirit. Another image is descent: Christ himself, through the Spirit, descends to be united with the believer. Another summative image is power: all this is accomplished by the Spirit, without which no sacramental union would be possible. Calvin does not attempt a precise account of the union of believer to Christ. Rather, he mines a range of images in order to portray the mystery of grace in the meal.

Although Stephenson finds the recent ecumenical language of Christ's "personal presence" to be a poor substitute for the classical language of Christ's "bodily presence," I welcome this conversation. Stephenson and I differ on whether this ecumenical dialogue has presented the Christian community with a step forward in unity. A confession of the personal presence of Christ in the Lord's Supper is able to recognize all the actions of the feast as filled with the presence of Christ. The words of institution, the elements themselves, the actions of giving and receiving, the thanksgiving—all of these are means by which God graces us with the presence of Christ through the Spirit.

A Baptist Response

I will do my best to look past the rhetoric of John Stephenson's essay and instead examine its substance. That is not easy. The tone, if not the actual language, is offensive to me and, I dare say, to most non-Missouri Synod Lutheran Christians. I do wonder if this essay represents the best of Lutheran thinking about the Lord's Supper. I have met and talked with many Lutheran theologians who would disagree with Stephenson's claims about the similarities between the "orthodox Lutheran" understanding of the Lord's Supper and Roman Catholic transubstantiation.

I doubt that Luther can rightly be held up as the norm for right Christian thinking about everything. Not only did his theology develop and change over time; it also contained elements about which most, if not all, Lutherans are ashamed. Luther's anti-Semitism and his urging the nobles to slay the peasants are among these. Just because Luther said it, in other words, does not make it the only orthodox Lutheran belief. Stephenson chooses to marginalize Melanchthon, but other Lutherans consider Melanchthon to be a great hero of the Lutheran tradition.

Many Lutherans and other Christians will be deeply offended and dismayed by the implication that any view of the Lord's Supper other than Stephenson's implies an "adoptionist" Christology. If I may be allowed to say so, this claim is simply wrongheaded, and it perpetuates unnecessary divisions among equally orthodox Christians.

If Jesus meant "This is my body, . . . this is my blood" literally, then the incarnation would be insecure. Luther's (and Stephenson's) interpretation of these words implies that while Jesus was standing with the disciples at the Last Supper, he was also in the bread and wine. Zwingli was right: Jesus was speaking metaphorically. It is the only way to make sense of the scene. A Christ who was both in the human body and outside of it by being in and with and under the very bread and wine he held—such a Christ would not be genuinely incarnate. The incarnation would be a charade. That is the trouble with the *communicatio idiomatum*. It is inconsistent with true incarnation. The Lutheran kenotic theologians were right.

Reformed and free-church Protestants are not dismayed at the Missouri Synod's closed Communion. We are not dying to participate in their Eucharistic fellowship. We are just puzzled as to why different understandings of the Supper should divide Christians.

As I read Stephenson's description of the Lutheran view of the Lord's Supper, I do not see it as a via media between the Catholic and Reformed views. It is squarely in the Catholic category, even if the language of transubstantiation is not used. That will come as a surprise and dismay to Reformed and free-church Protestants. From our perspective, the distance between Catholic sacramental theology and Protestant sacramental theology is narrow, if it exists at all, when Stephenson speaks about baptism and Eucharist as salvific without mentioning the necessity of faith. Does he believe it takes effect *ex opere operato?* That remains unclear.

In sum, I found Stephenson's essay on the Lord's Supper to be bewildering. It goes far beyond "real presence" to implying that human persons actually masticate the flesh and swallow the blood of Jesus in the Lord's Supper. Well, let that branch of Lutherans believe it, but as Stephenson acknowledges, even most Lutherans cannot stomach it. And nowhere does Scripture require it unless one uses an overly literalistic hermeneutic that would also require cutting off hands and plucking out eyes.

A PENTECOSTAL RESPONSE

Whereas the Roman Catholic writer Brother Jeffrey Gros devotes much of his space to the consideration of the communion and the unity of the church, John Stephenson, writing from a Lutheran perspective, sets the discussion firmly in a christological focus: "A Lutheran theologian cannot regard these opening reflections on Christology as out of place in an essay devoted to the rite that the old Lutherans usually termed the sacrament of the altar or the Lord's Supper." I find fascinating and helpful the tracing of some major christological trajectories, beginning from the church fathers and focusing on the Reformation debates regarding their implications for sacramentology. While focusing on Christology, the presentation also does not miss the communion (fellowship) aspect of Lutheran sacramentology, even though that could have been more in focus, especially in light of the recent theological reflection on Communion produced by the Lutheran World Federation.

As an ecumenist, I found highly interesting and helpful Stephenson's claim that "the different ways in which Lutherans and Roman Catholics articulate the real presence are in themselves not necessarily church-divisive"—provided, as the author further states, that the Eucharist Communion cannot happen until key doctrinal issues are resolved. As a Pentecostal and free-church Christian, I was interested in Stephenson's observation that, even though "Luther was right and Zwingli was wrong," when it comes to the understanding of the Lord's presence at the Eucharist, "at the same time I must ruefully admit the accuracy of the Anglican bishop Michael Marshall's quip that, while Luther won the battle, Zwingli went on to win the war. After all, with the exception of perhaps one-third of Anglicans, Zwingli has rather much swept the field of world Protestantism." As revealed by my essay in this book and the discussion of the Baptist view of the Lord's Supper by Roger Olson, much of the free-church tradition is permeated by the "symbolic" Zwinglian understanding—for better or for worse!

While the essays in this compendium are supposed to represent a given tradition assigned to the particular author, they are not supposed to be encyclopedic accounts of everything about that tradition. Even then, I was wondering if Lutherans coming from another (in this case, American) brand of Lutheranism would have wanted to have more treatment on the diversity of Lutheran views and practices with regard to, say, intercommunion. At least for one raised in a country that is probably the world's most Lutheran country (Finland) and trained in Helsinki by Lutheran mentors, this diversity is part of Lutheranism's contemporary ethos. Yet as an outsider to the Lutheran tradition, I cannot help but reflect on how Lutherans from different contexts than Stephenson's setting may receive these kinds of remarks: "The statements of Luther and the Confessions . . . align orthodox Lutherans with the Roman and Orthodox churches with respect to the Blessed Sacrament and, on this point at least, erect an insuperable wall of separation between orthodox Lutheranism and the wide world of Protestantism."

3

THE REFORMED VIEW

Leanne Van Dyk

Each week, Christian believers celebrate the Lord's Supper all over the world in their own language, context, culture and liturgy. Although divisions within the church are a deep burden for the body of Christ, the long continuity of sacramental celebrations, in the multiplicity of forms, gives visible witness to the work of the Holy Spirit. From its beginning the Reformed tradition has been an international movement, marked by diversity and a range of theological options. In the sixteenth and seventeenth centuries, urban centers of Reformed activity flourished in France, Switzerland, Hungary, the Czech Republic, Italy, the Netherlands, England and Scotland. In following centuries the Reformed tradition has found root in a wide variety of cultures and contexts, including South Korea, the Philippines, South Africa, Brazil, North America and India, among others. From the earliest years of the Reformed tradition, one area of diversity included the theology and practices of the Lord's Supper.

The deep differences in Reformed understandings of the Lord's Supper can be traced back to early Reformed founders, each with their own conceptual and ecclesial framework. The tensions that existed between the Protestant and the Catholic, as well as between the various communities of Protestants themselves, often focused on the sacraments. Debate was so vigorous partly because both baptism and the Lord's Supper pull in many other theological issues, including Christology and ecclesiology. In addition, political tensions heightened the polemics, and ambitions often played out regionally. Contemporary Reformed believers might wonder why these old arguments and issues have relevance for faith today. A historical survey of the early Reformed communities gives us the opportunity not only to claim the tradition that continues to form us, but also to see the sacramental distinctions set in real communities of faith. Careful attention to and respect for the early sources of the Reformed tradition do not require a stiff adherence to classic sources. Such attention can, instead, give vitality to a fresh appropriation of sacramental expressions of faith. There is heartening evidence that such sacramental renewal is happening in many places in the Reformed tradition. Often a discovery of Reformed and broadly classical sources have encouraged this renewal.

Historians and theologians of the Reformed tradition have suggested a number of paradigms that group and characterize features of this sacramental variety. This chapter will explore the sacramental theology of several important early Reformed leaders and offer an identifying term for each. The Lord's Supper doctrine of John Calvin will be affirmed as the most vital and fruitful for contemporary Reformed traditions.

The three early Reformed leaders who formulated distinct Reformed Eucharistic theology were Ulrich Zwingli, Heinrich Bullinger and John Calvin. The clear differences between these three give rise to the observation that differentiation on Lord's Supper theology in the Reformed tradition is much broader than within the Lutheran or Catholic traditions. Although the Reformed tradition demonstrates some continuity and coherence on central theological claims and instincts, there is a significant range of meanings with respect to the Lord's Supper.

The Lord's Supper doctrine of Ulrich Zwingli, pastor of the reforming church in Zurich from early in the 1520s until his untimely death in 1531, can be described as "memorialism." In marked contrast to the Roman Catholic tradition of his youth and training, Zwingli proposed a symbolic or representational approach.[1] The bread and the wine indicate a spiritual reality, and the Holy Spirit is active in the sacrament as the Spirit

---

[1]Ulrich Zwingli, "On the Lord's Supper," in *Zwingli and Bullinger*, ed. G. W. Bromiley, Library of Christian Classics 23 (London: SCM Press, 1953), p. 225.

is in the whole life of the community of believers. But the sacrament is primarily a sign that points beyond itself to the reality of the risen and ascended Christ.

The separation of sign and reality is a key feature of Zwingli's sacramental theology. These *must* be separate because the sovereignty and freedom of God is not bound to the sacramental elements. In no way must it be said that God could not act apart from them and must act in them.[2] One Zwingli commentator says, "The sign was one thing, and in itself it was only a sign. The thing signified was quite another, and it had no necessary connection with the sign except that it was represented by it."[3] In a striking analogy, another commentator remarks that, for Zwingli, the sacramental signs are signs of holy things, "but they are no more what they signify than the word 'ape' when written down is an ape."[4]

Other Reformers differed sharply with Zwingli's understanding of sign and reality. About twenty years later, writing in 1540, John Calvin challenged the separation of the sacramental elements and the reality of Jesus Christ: "The sacraments of the Lord should not and cannot be at all separated from their reality and substance."[5] For Zwingli, however, a representational understanding follows the most direct meaning of Scripture as well as patristic authorities.[6] In a 1524 letter to Matthew Alber, he writes, "I think the hinge of the matter is to be found in a very short syllable, namely, in the word 'is,' the meaning of which is not always given by 'is' but sometimes by 'signifies.'"[7] He goes on: "Put 'signifies' for 'is' here and you have, 'Take, eat; this signifies my body which is given for you.' Then the meaning will certainly be, 'Take, eat; for this which I bid

[2]W. Peter Stephens, *The Theology of Huldrych Zwingli* (Oxford: Clarendon, 1986), p. 250.

[3]Bromiley, in his introduction to Zwingli's "On the Lord's Supper," in *Zwingli and Bullinger*, p. 182.

[4]Stephens, *Theology of Zwingli*, p. 189.

[5]John Calvin, "Short Treatise on the Lord's Supper," in *Tracts and Treatises on the Reformation of the Church*, vol. 2, *On the Doctrine and Worship of the Church*, trans. Henry Beveridge (Grand Rapids: Eerdmans, 1958), p. 172.

[6]In reference to the church fathers, Zwingli says, "They use exactly the same speech as we do, for they call the bread and wine the body and blood of Christ, although what they really mean is that they are the representation and memorial of his body and blood"; from "On the Lord's Supper," in Bromiley, *Zwingli and Bullinger*, p. 234.

[7]*Selected Writings of Huldrych Zwingli*, vol. 2, *In Search of True Religion*, ed. and trans. H. Wayne Pipkin (Allison Park, Penn.: Pickwick Publications, 1984), p. 138.

you do will signify to you or remind you of my body which presently is to be given for you.'"[8] These statements confirm Zwingli's representational understanding of the elements; they point beyond themselves to bring to heart and mind the reality of salvation.

Although Zwingli advocates a representational memorialism for the Lord's Supper, it is a mistake to conclude that he holds a "mere" memorialism. He has no wish to deny the divine presence of Jesus Christ in the Supper or in the community of faith. For Zwingli, the sacrament is much more than a "calling to mind" of the person of Jesus Christ. "The Supper cannot be merely a commemorative rite when the one commemorated is himself present and active amongst those who keep the feast."[9] Thus the notion that the Lord's Supper was simply a symbolic commemoration does not do justice to Zwingli's full doctrine.

Yet Zwingli's separation of sign and reality sets the primary action of the sacrament in the believer. In his 1526 treatise "On the Lord's Supper," he says, "And when we poor creatures observe this act of thanksgiving amongst ourselves, we all confess that we are of those who believe in the Lord Jesus Christ."[10] Again, Zwingli insists that Jesus Christ instituted the Lord's Supper not only so that we might never forget Christ's death for our sakes, but also so "that we might publicly attest it with praise and thanksgiving, joining together for the greater magnifying and proclaiming of the matter in the eating and drinking of the sacrament."[11] The believer observes, remembers, attests, proclaims; these are the primary sacramental actions.

Zwingli's memorialism is an implication of his Christology. Like other Reformed leaders, he puts a strong emphasis on the incarnation and ascension. Jesus Christ is no longer present: he has ascended in his resurrected human nature and sits at the right hand of God. Thus Zwingli tries to articulate how Christ is spiritually active in but not present in the Lord's Supper. "Inasmuch as he is man, Christ is not to be expected in the world

---

[8]Ibid., p. 139.
[9]Bromiley, in his introduction to Zwingli's "On the Lord's Supper," in *Zwingli and Bullinger*, p. 183.
[10]Zwingli, "On the Lord's Supper," in ibid., p. 235.
[11]Ibid., p. 234.

with a natural, essential and corporal presence, but only with a spiritual and sacramental."[12]

The confessing and attesting activity of the believer is done in a communal context; the church gives public expression of faith and gratitude. In a 1525 letter to Rhegius, Zwingli says, "Therefore our Eucharist is a visible assembling of the church, in which we eat and drink bread and wine as symbols, that we may be reminded of those things which Christ has done for us."[13] For Zwingli, the bread and wine of the Lord's Supper is a representational memorial by which the community publicly gives thanksgiving for the saving death of Christ, confesses faith in Christ, and pledges obedience and service to Christ. "To eat the body of Christ spiritually is equivalent to trusting with heart and soul upon the mercy and goodness of God through Christ."[14] The actual sacramental eating and drinking are to receive Christ with faith and gratitude; they affirm and acknowledge the grace of God in Jesus Christ that has already been offered.

The question of what sacramental eating and drinking mean theologically and pastorally has been a main area of dispute across the Christian tradition and between Reformed leaders as well. Zwingli carefully marks off his view from the alternatives: "Now for some time there has been bitter contention amongst us as to what the sacraments or signs themselves either do or can do in the Supper. Our adversaries allege that the sacraments give faith, mediate the natural body of Christ, and enable us to eat it as substantially present. But we have good cause to think otherwise."[15] Zwingli carefully avoids language that both Bullinger and Calvin would, in later years, affirm. The sacraments do not give faith or mediate the presence of Christ. Only the Holy Spirit can give saving faith. The sacraments do give faith, but only "historical faith," as Zwingli puts it, just like celebrations, monuments and statues give "historical faith," or a reminder of some past event.

If the Lord's Supper does not confer grace or make Jesus Christ present, what is the use of the sacrament? For Zwingli, the sacraments are

---

[12] Zwingli, "An Exposition of the Faith," in ibid., p. 257.

[13] Stephens, *Theology of Zwingli*, p. 240.

[14] Zwingli, "An Exposition of the Faith," in Bromiley, *Zwingli and Bullinger*, p. 258.

[15] Ibid., p. 260.

efficacious in a number of ways: Jesus Christ has instituted them, and so they are sacred. They confirm historical events. They represent sacred events. They are a support to faith. And they function as a promise of obedience for the community.[16] They thus are means by which the community calls to mind and heart the truth of the gospel.

There is little doubt that the approach to the Lord's Supper expressed by Ulrich Zwingli was taken up in large part by the subsequent Reformed tradition. Many generations of Reformed believers have assumed that the Lord's Supper is a memorial act, a way to remember the death and resurrection of Jesus Christ, an encouragement to gratitude and service. Zwingli's influence has been significant in Reformed theology and practice.

Zwingli was killed in 1531 in the Battle of Kappel, a military skirmish between a Roman Catholic militia and the Protestant militia of Zurich over political control of the territory. Next in that leading pastoral office was Heinrich Bullinger, whose Lord's Supper doctrine can be characterized as "parallelism." He served the Zurich church as a reforming pastor from 1531–1575, a long pastorate of forty-four years.

Bullinger's understanding of the Lord's Supper developed over his impressively long ministry in Zurich. He had early conversations in the 1520s with Zwingli on the sacrament and a long debate with Calvin in the 1540s, during which time his mature doctrine developed. Like Zwingli, Bullinger understood the sacrament as symbolic and representational. However, like Calvin (see below), Bullinger affirmed the active role of Jesus Christ in self-giving grace at the Table. In his last set of sermons, collected as the *Decades,* he says, "The supper of the Lord is an holy action instituted unto the church from God, wherein the Lord, by the setting of bread and wine before us at the banquet, doth certify unto us his promise and communion, and sheweth unto us his gifts and layeth them before our senses."[17] The affirmation of divine gracious activity in the Lord's Supper signals an important difference from Zwingli, who understood the congregation, in its acts of dedication and gratitude, to be the primary subjects in the sacrament.

---

[16] Ibid., pp. 262-65.

[17] Heinrich Bullinger, *Decades,* §V.9.403, quoted in Paul Rorem, *Calvin and Bullinger on the Lord's Supper* (Bramcote and Nottingham: Grove Books, 1989), p. 15.

It was, however, the extended debate between Bullinger and Calvin that pressured both leaders to articulate precisely their Lord's Supper doctrine. A series of treatises, letters and meetings ultimately produced the Consensus Tigurinus of 1549, a key Reformed document of sacramental theology that won the assent, even if guarded, of both Calvin and Bullinger.

Several key issues emerged in their careful debate. One is the central relationship between sign and signified already identified in Zwingli. For Bullinger, like Zwingli, the sacramental signs are not connected to the thing signified. The sign is a sign, not an instrument or channel of grace. This does not mean that they are useless. In a careful attempt to articulate what sacramental signs are not and what they are, Bullinger says: "Therefore they that are partakers of the sacraments do not receive nothing, as these say, unless the institution of God be esteemed as nothing. He instituted sacraments to be testimonies of his grace, and seals of the truth of his promises."[18] The language of "testimony" is important for Bullinger. The sacramental signs are not mere symbols that point to something else, but rather are analogies of the gracious activity of God. These signs do not themselves, however, confer grace. Sacramental action and divine action are separate. They are related but not joined.

The term *parallelism* is helpful in understanding how Bullinger relates the sign to God's activity. He says that just as we eat the bread and drink the wine in a physical manner, so the Spirit unites us to Christ. "As bread nourishes and strengthens man, and gives him ability to labor; so the body of Christ, eaten by faith, feeds and satisfies the soul of man."[19] The eating of sacramental elements does not in itself confer grace, but the eating of the sacramental elements "parallels" the analogous divine action. For Bullinger, the bread and wine are a testimony to divine grace, not an instrument of divine grace. In the Second Helvetic Confession (1564), Bullinger expresses this same parallel conceptual frame. The contrast of "inward" and "outward" is used to portray his parallelism:

And this is *visibly* represented by this sacrament *outwardly* through the ministers, and, as it were, presented to our eyes to be seen, which

---

[18] Bullinger, *Decades*, §V.7.314, quoted in Rorem, *Calvin and Bullinger*, p. 25.
[19] Bullinger, *Decades*, §V.7.329, quoted in Rorem, *Calvin and Bullinger*, p. 26.

is *invisibly* wrought by the Holy Spirit *inwardly* in the soul. Bread is
outwardly offered by the minister, and words of the Lord are heard. . . .
At the same time by the work of Christ through the Holy Spirit, they also
inwardly receive the flesh and blood of the Lord.[20]

The parallelism of inward and outward, of visible and invisible, is clear
for Bullinger. The sacramental signs correspond to simultaneous divine
activity. This understanding of the sacramental elements was one of the
central issues of debate between Calvin and Bullinger in the 1540s. Their
series of letters, personal visits and lengthy treatises did not settle this
question. The parallelism of Bullinger contrasts with the instrumentalism of Calvin and marks a deep underlying difference in their sacramental visions. For Bullinger, the sacramental signs testify to God's gracious
gifts; for Calvin, the signs are instruments of the Holy Spirit and reliable
means of grace.

This difference in understanding the relationship between sign and
thing signified bequeathed to the subsequent Reformed tradition some
significant ambiguities that are even deeper than that already indicated by
Zwingli. Rorem summarizes these differences:

> Does a given Reformed statement of faith consider the Lord's Supper as
> testimony, an analogy, a parallel, even a simultaneous parallel to the inter-
> nal workings of God's grace in granting communion with Christ? If so, the
> actual ancestor may be Heinrich Bullinger, Zwingli's successor in Zurich.
> Or does it explicitly identify the Supper as the very instrument or means
> through which God offers and confers the grace of full communion with
> Christ's body? The lineage would then go back to John Calvin.[21]

John Calvin is certainly the one who towers above the other early
leaders of Reformed communities. He engaged in vigorous conversation
with both Lutheran and Reformed leaders over the Lord's Supper, and
in these polemical exchanges he developed his mature doctrine. There
is discernible development in Calvin's understanding of the Lord's Supper from early to late in his ministry. One Calvin scholar summarizes:

---

[20] *The Book of Confessions of the Presbyterian Church (USA)* (Louisville, Ky.: Office of the General
Assembly, 2002), §5.196 <www.pcusa.org/oga/publications/boc.pdf>.
[21] Rorem, *Calvin and Bullinger,* pp. 54-55.

"We will see Calvin move from denying the Eucharist as an instrument of grace to affirming it as such. We will see Calvin develop a notion of substantial partaking of the true body and blood of Christ over his career; an emphasis that is practically absent, even denied, in his earliest teaching."[22] As a result of this development, Calvin's view is best described as "instrumentalism," the view that the elements and actions of the Lord's Supper accomplish what they say. Calvin's statement of instrumentalism is unmistakable in his 1541 "Short Treatise on the Lord's Supper," where he says, "It is with good reason then that the bread is called the body, since it not only represents but also presents it to us."[23]

Calvin has three primary affirmations on the Lord's Supper.[24] First, Calvin affirms the divine origin of all goodness, all graces, all gifts. The Lord's Supper is a gift of God for the purpose of supporting and nourishing the faith of the community of believers. Because God is like a caring and attentive parent, God provides for us in ways that we both need and can receive.[25] We are creaturely; therefore, the creaturely, material reality of the sacramental elements is uniquely suited for us. The Eucharist brings to our faltering faith the riches of God's love. Calvin uses a variety of images to convey the gift character of the sacraments; they are like pictures, seals, exercises, promises, visible words, mirrors and pillars. For instance, he says that the sacraments are like mirrors into which we look to see the riches of God's grace, which God "lavishes upon us."[26]

Calvin's repeated affirmation of the Lord's Supper as a loving gift of God to the people of faith displays the pastoral heart of his theology. The polemical nature of the debates between Calvin and a wide variety of opponents in his life can obscure this central concern. Calvin is eager to comfort and encourage faltering hearts with the confidence that God

---

[22]Thomas J. Davis, *The Clearest Promises of God: The Development of Calvin's Eucharistic Teaching* (New York: AMS Press, 1995), pp. 7-8.

[23]John Calvin, "Short Treatise on the Lord's Supper," in Beveridge, *Tracts and Treatises*, 2:171-72.

[24]For a fuller treatment of these themes, see Leanne Van Dyk, "The Gifts of God for the People of God: Christian Feminism and Sacramental Theology," in *Feminist and Womanist Essays in Reformed Dogmatics*, ed. Amy Plantinga Pauw and Serene Jones (Louisville, Ky.: Westminster John Knox Press, 2006), pp. 204-20.

[25]John Calvin, *Institutes of the Christian Religion*, ed. John T. McNeill, trans. Ford Lewis Battles (Philadelphia: Westminster Press, 1960), §4.17.1.

[26]Ibid., §4.14.6.

has spread before us a spiritual banquet in the Lord's Supper and bids us come.[27] This is a gift with a promise and purpose: God wishes to confirm, to testify, to seal, to remind, to assure us of all the benefits of Christ.[28]

Second, the Lord's Supper always points beyond itself to Jesus Christ. Calvin emphasizes the deep connections between Scripture, sacrament, and Christ. He explains, "Therefore, let it be regarded as a settled principle that the sacraments have the same office as the Word of God: to offer and set forth Christ to us, and in him the treasures of heavenly grace."[29] Hughes Oliphant Old expresses this unity of the word of God simply: "Sermon and Supper go together."[30]

Calvin's emphasis that Jesus Christ is a living presence in word and sacrament is at the heart of his understanding of the gospel. He begins book three of the *Institutes* by asserting, "We must understand that as long as Christ remains outside of us, and we are separated from him, all that he has suffered and done for the salvation of the human race remains useless and of no value for us."[31] The Holy Spirit bridges this great historical and ontological divide between human creatures and Jesus Christ, bringing into union the believer and Christ. In the sacrament of baptism, this union is initiated; in the sacrament of the Lord's Supper, it is confirmed and sustained.

How Jesus Christ is present to us in the Lord's Supper is one of the deep mysteries of sacramental theology, as well as one of the liveliest points of dispute in the early Reformed tradition. Calvin insists that Christ is present to us in his flesh and blood in the sacrament. He professes the inadequacy of human words to express this great truth, but nonetheless insists that this union is between the actual, real, risen Christ and the believer. He says, "Nothing remains but to break forth in wonder at this mystery, which plainly neither the mind is able to conceive nor the tongue to express."[32] The believer receives the body of Christ in the Lord's Supper in ways that we can scarcely comprehend, but yet confess. It is not enough

---

[27] Ibid., §4.17.1.

[28] Ibid., §4.17.5.

[29] Ibid., §4.14.17.

[30] Hughes Oliphant Old, *Worship: Reformed According to Scripture* (Louisville, Ky.: Westminster John Knox Press, 2002), p. 128.

[31] Calvin *Institutes* §3.1.1.

[32] Ibid., §4.17.7.

to state that Christ is the bread of life by *believing* in Christ, by "mere knowledge."[33] Calvin says instead "that his flesh is truly food, and his blood truly drink, and by these foods believers are nourished unto eternal life."[34] The flesh of Christ nourishes and restores us like an "inexhaustible fountain that pours into us the life springing forth."[35] The insistence of Calvin that the sacramental sign truly conveys what it signifies—Jesus Christ—is a prominent feature of Calvin's Lord's Supper doctrine. He states this in strong terms as early as 1541 and never backs away from it:

> We must confess, then, that . . . the internal substance of the sacrament is conjoined with the visible signs. . . . We have good cause to be satisfied, when we understand that Jesus Christ gives us in the Supper the proper substance of his body and blood.[36]

Third, the prominent role of the Holy Spirit in Calvin's Lord's Supper doctrine is striking. For Calvin, everything depends on the Spirit. Neither sermon nor sacrament will point to Jesus Christ without the action of the Holy Spirit. Calvin says simply that "they are of no further benefit unless the Holy Spirit accompanies them."[37] He acknowledges the enormity of the claim that our souls are fed by the flesh and blood of Christ and that we are united to Christ. But, once again appealing to the incomprehensibility of God, he says:

> Even though it seems unbelievable that Christ's flesh, separated from us by such great distance, penetrates to us, so that it becomes our food, let us remember how far the secret power of the Holy Spirit towers above all our senses, and how foolish it is to wish to measure his immeasurableness by our measure. That, then, our mind does not comprehend, let faith conceive: that the Spirit truly unites things separated in space.[38]

---

[33] Ibid., §4.17.5.

[34] Ibid., §4.17.8. See also the French Confession, written by Calvin in 1562, which expresses Calvin's fully developed Lord's Supper theology: in §38 this confession says that Christ "fails not to give us life in himself, to dwell in us, to provide for us and make us partakers of the substance of his body and his blood, by the incomprehensible virtue of his Spirit"; in Beveridge, *Tracts and Treatises*, 2:161.

[35] Calvin *Institutes* §4.17.9.

[36] John Calvin, "Short Treatise," in Beveridge, *Tracts and Treatises*, 2:172-73.

[37] Calvin *Institutes* §4.14.17.

[38] Ibid., §4.17.10.

The challenge of accounting for the separation between Christ and the believer is particularly acute for the Reformed theological tradition. The Reformed tradition does not accept the Lutheran ubiquity doctrine, which states that Christ's human nature is present everywhere in the world.[39] Nor does it accept the classic Roman Catholic theory of transubstantiation, which explains that Christ's true body has locally replaced the essence of the sacramental elements.[40] The distinctive emphasis in the Reformed tradition on Jesus' ascension rules out these options. So how is Jesus Christ present in the sacrament? We have seen that Zwingli answered this question by proposing a memorial understanding of Christ's presence: Christ is in heaven, and we bring to heart and mind in the Supper what Christ has accomplished for us. Bullinger answered this question by asserting that as we partake of the sacrament, so Christ by the Spirit is made present to us. Calvin made a bolder sacramental claim, that although Christ is in heaven, we are nourished in the Lord's Supper by his body and blood as the food of our souls, united to him in the Spirit.

To support this sacramental approach, Calvin used at least two supports. He frequently used the image of "ascent" to portray the mystery of the union of Christ and the believer.[41] Furthermore, he reflected carefully on the precise meaning of the word *is* in Christ's words "This is my body."[42] The Marburg Colloquy of 1529, where Zwingli and Luther argued vigorously over the meaning of this same freighted sacramental word, led to no Lutheran-Reformed agreement. Although Luther insisted on a simple and strong equation between sign and reality, Calvin, writing many years later in the *Institutes,* understood *is* as a figure of speech that is uniquely, though partially, able to convey mystery. "This *is* my body" means, in effect, "This *is* the whole incarnate, risen and ascended Jesus Christ along with the grace that God promises you in this feast."

---

[39]Calvin rejects consubstantiation and ubiquity in the French Confession, §36 (1562); in Beveridge, *Tracts and Treatises,* 2:160.

[40]In the French Confession, §35 (1562), Calvin likewise rejects transubstantiation, claiming that it does not recognize the union with Christ that we have through the bread and wine *as* bread and wine; in Beveridge, *Tracts and Treatises,* 2:159.

[41]Calvin *Institutes* §§4.17.2; 4.17.15; 4.17.16; 4.17.18; 4.17.31

[42]Ibid., §4.17.21.

Christ is present in bread and wine, and we are united with him through the gracious initiative of God, not because of the worthiness of the recipient or the minister. Although faith is required to receive the gifts of the Holy Spirit, God is faithful to give the gift of Jesus Christ to believers when they receive this gift with thankful and sincere hearts. This means that the Lord's Supper is not under the control of the church, the minister or the people. Instead, the grace of the Lord's Supper is always a fresh gift of God through the Holy Spirit.

The three emphases of Calvin's view of the Lord's Supper just noted also highlight the trinitarian character of his Lord's Supper doctrine. The gift character of the Supper highlights the gracious action of God, the loving and generous Father. The sacrament presents Christ and unites us with Christ, the "only food of our soul."[43] The Holy Spirit is highlighted in uniting us to Christ and commissioning the sacramental elements to convey the grace that they indicate.

The differences between the Reformed leaders Zwingli, Bullinger and Calvin are significant. Zwingli can best be described as holding a "memorialism" view, Bullinger a "parallelism" view, and Calvin an "instrumentalism" view of the Lord's Supper. Although these differences mean that the Reformed tradition allows greater variety in sacramental understanding than either the Lutheran tradition or the Roman Catholic tradition, there are also common affirmations they share. The broad Reformed tradition affirms the importance of faith in receiving the grace of the sacrament. They agree that the Lord's Supper is an expression and continuation of God's covenant with God's people. They all affirm the communal implications of the Supper and stress sacramental communion and fellowship. In his history of Reformed worship, Hughes Oliphant Old says, "The sharing of the bread and the cup by the whole people of God becomes the heart of the service."[44] The community is built up and nourished in the sharing of the Lord's Supper.

The voice of the Reformed tradition concerning the Lord's Supper is not limited to Zwingli, Bullinger and Calvin. Many other important voices join in the conversation. The nineteenth-century American theologian John

---

[43] Ibid., §4.17.1.
[44] Old, *Worship*, p. 127.

Williamson Nevin, founder of the Reformed theological tradition known as Mercersburg theology, considered John Calvin to be the best exponent of the meaning of the Lord's Supper. Nevin differentiated between a number of sacramental options and endorsed Calvin's: "We communicate, in the Lord's Supper, not with the divine promise merely, not with the thought of Christ alone, not with the recollection simply of what he has done and suffered for us, not with the lively present sense alone of his all-sufficient, all-glorious salvation; but with the living Savior himself in the fullness of his glorified person made present to us for the purpose by the power of the Holy Spirit."[45]

The global character of the Reformed tradition also expresses the Reformed doctrine of the Lord's Supper in a wide variety of ways. Reformed communities that are engaged in liturgical retrieval have lifted up the liturgy as formative for the believing community. Reformed communities that are struggling with entrenched patterns of oppression or injustice find the Lord's Supper to be a source of both God's encouragement and God's mandate for reconciliation. What the Reformed tradition has always emphasized, from its earliest roots to its contemporary diversity, are both the generosity and encouragement of God in the Supper and the communal and ethical implications of the Lord's Supper.

The pastoral effects of the Lord's Supper are indicated by many voices in the Reformed tradition. Zwingli highlights the importance of gratitude in the sacrament. Calvin uses the central image of nourishment. Pastoral effects are further identified by Calvin in the Genevan Catechism of 1541. He refers to an intensification of grace, a concentrated experience of God's grace in the Lord's Supper. Similarly, the "Short Treatise on the Lord's Supper," also written in 1541, affirms that "in the Supper we have more ample certainty, and fuller enjoyment of [grace]."[46]

If the Lord's Supper offers a concentrated experience of God's grace, all the moments and actions of the sacrament are weighted with significance. God's grace is not limited to the partaking of the elements themselves or

---

[45]John Williamson Nevin, *The Mystical Presence: A Vindication of the Reformed or Calvinistic Doctrine of the Holy Eucharist* (Philadelphia: S. R. Fisher, 1867), p. 58.

[46]John Calvin, Genevan Catechism, in Beveridge, *Tracts and Treatises,* 2:90; "Short Treatise on the Lord's Supper," in Beveridge, *Tracts and Treatises,* 2:169.

to the words of institution. Rather, the whole liturgical and communal worship conveys the grace of God. This means that Reformed congregations will take care with the liturgy, the visual elements, the sensory context of the Supper. Music matters, the Communion table matters, the music and art and movement matter. How the congregation prepares for and responds to the sacrament matter. Care in all these will form an attentive congregation, eager to receive God's grace.

One of the characteristics of the Reformed tradition is recognition of how grateful response ripples out from the worship service to all of life. Calvin is particularly eloquent on this:

> We shall benefit very much from the Sacrament if this thought is impressed and engraved upon our minds: that none of the [brothers or sisters] can be injured, despised, rejected, abused, or in any way offended by us, without at the same time, injuring, despising, and abusing Christ by the wrongs we do; . . . that we ought to take the same care of our [brothers' or sisters'] bodies as we take of our own; for they are members of our body; and that as no part of our body is touched by any feeling of pain which is not spread among all the rest, so we ought not to allow a [brother or sister] to be affected by any evil, without being touched with compassion for him.[47]

In short, the Lord's Supper is "the bond of love," as Augustine once said; it unites us not only to Jesus Christ, but also to one another in the community of faith. Sacramental virtues in the Reformed tradition include care for the sick, injured and despised of society; they include attention to children and elderly; they include support of just laws and policies that reflect awareness of economic and political disparities. Sacramental virtues in the Reformed tradition explicitly affirm that being united with Christ is a reality so deep and broad that all areas of life are implicated. Because the Lord's Supper is a gift of grace, believers gathered in community ought joyfully to anticipate the gift, always in confidence and joy that it will be given.

The Lord's Supper liturgy in the Reformed Church in America begins with the words "Beloved in the Lord Jesus Christ, the holy Supper which

---

[47]Calvin *Institutes* §4.17.38. Bracketed words replace "brethren" in the Westminster Press (1960) edition.

we are about to celebrate is a feast of remembrance, of communion, and of hope." These words set the sacrament in the wide expanse of God's gracious actions in past, present and future. We celebrate in remembrance for the past revelation of God throughout history and especially in Jesus Christ. We celebrate in communion by being united to Christ through the power of the Holy Spirit. We celebrate in hope by glimpsing in the sacrament a foretaste of the great heavenly banquet, when all saints and angels together will join in the praise of God. In this way, the congregation truly receives the gifts of God for the people of God.

A Roman Catholic Response

A word of appreciation to Leanne Van Dyk for outlining the contribution of three important Reformation figures, clarifying the role of the Holy Spirit in Reformed theology and opening up the formative dimension of Eucharist worship.

There is a general recognition that Calvin is probably the most articulate among the Reformers and one of the great systematic theologians of the era. However, some among the non-Reformed theological community also have a lack of enthusiasm for his personality and his contribution. A clear and positive view of Calvin and his colleagues is important for all serious Christians.

Bullinger's contribution is important, especially because of the durability of his covenant theology in the American Protestant culture and spirituality. Consideration of Martin Bucer's contribution to Eucharist reflection is also needed for a complete picture of sixteenth-century debates and the evolution of those ideas in the worship life of the churches.

Yet issues raised by the sign and signified, as well as the theology of symbolism, remain important areas of discussion, as I observe in my paper. Reformed-Catholic dialogue has much more work to do together to resolve our sacramental differences on the Supper. Certainly most Catholics are surprised at the seriousness with which Calvin in particular takes the biblical teaching of Paul on Christ's presence in the Supper.

Often those who do not study the Reformed Eucharistic theology carefully, including many members of churches bearing these confessional commitments, judge the affirmation of a spiritual presence as diminishing the realism of Reformed sacramental understanding. However, Van Dyk recalls the high pneumatology that accompanies Reformed high Christology.

In the modern ecumenical discussions, the conversations with the Orthodox over their understanding of epiclesis *(epiklēsis)* and the role of the Holy Spirit in the community, in the Supper, and in making present the body and blood of the Savior—all have helped to build bridges of understanding, even if not yet sufficient consensus in faith to make sharing at the Lord's Table possible. However, these Reformed, Orthodox and, more recently, Pentecostal voices have helped to renew the trinitarian perspective in our understanding of God's action in the community, especially the Eucharistic assembly.

Finally, I am most appreciative of Van Dyk's emphasis on the role of "the sacrament in the wide expanse of God's gracious actions in past, present and future." The language Catholics use for this role is the "source and summit" of the Christian life. However, it is easy to misunderstand such a phrase as though it points to a ritual divorced from a Eucharistic/thankful way of living in Christ.

It is necessary to understand "liturgy as formative for the believing community," and not as an isolated action, ritual or object. Christians need to be formed for and by worship: their own worship, a knowledge of the worship traditions of others and their Christian claims, how they differ from one's own tradition, and hopes for reconciliation at the Lord's Table. (See <www.vatican.va/roman_curia/pontifical_councils/chrstuni/documents /rc_pc_chrstuni_doc_16031998_ecumenical-dimension_en.html>.)

A Lutheran Response

As Leanne Van Dyk summarizes the position(s) of those most properly labeled "Reformed," she lays her finger on Reformed "diversity" past and present, to which I react by asking, What happened to the apostolic command that we all "say the same thing" (*hina to auto legēte pantes,* 1 Cor 1:10) and be "of one mind" (*hina to auto phronēte,* Phil 2:2)? In order to express fellowship with one another in the church in general and at the altar in particular, we need to confess the same doctrine.

I cry "Argh!" as Van Dyk misrepresents Rome as teaching the Lord's "local" presence in his sacrament, and as she tars Luther and Lutheranism with the brush of "ubiquity." For while confessing the Lord's transcendent/immanent "omnipresence" according to his humanity, we do not identify this with his real, *definitive* presence on the altar. Moreover, the Lord's Word alone is the basis of our sacramental doctrine; "omnipresence" is merely an apologetic response to the Reformed objection that Jesus' body cannot be in heaven and in the sacrament at the same time.

Van Dyk gives a useful lesson in historical theology as she sets forth the differences between Zwingli's "memorialism," Bullinger's "parallelism" and Calvin's "instrumentalism." Calvin's famous treatise of 1541 comes closest to acknowledging the Lord's Supper as a means of grace, but in his very approach to the Lord's word and deed, Calvin uncannily recoils from Jesus' voice and from the body he holds in his hand for the feeding of his flock.

Of the three "Reformed" contributors, Van Dyk, as the actual Reformed spokesperson, establishes some common ground with traditional Lutheranism as she advocates liturgical dignity and decorum. She also speaks within the "catholic" tradition and in convincing fashion as she highlights the communal, moral impulse implicit within the sacramental gift (an aspect emphasized at times by Luther but oftentimes left unstressed by later Lutherans).

The Calvinist "instrumentalism" that she highlights is closer to Scripture and the church fathers than Zwingli's "separation of sign and reality" (but how may we separate what the Lord has verbally and thus actually joined together?). Yet Van Dyk spells out a common Reformed bottom line when she remarks that Zwingli "sets the primary action of the sacrament in the believer." But the holiness of the Old Testament sacrifices, which were true means of grace for the ancient people of God, resided primarily in the victims offered on the altar and only secondarily in the Israelites rendered holy by eating them. In the same way, the bread and wine supernaturally become the Lord's body and blood and are "most holy," imparting holiness to those who receive them in penitent faith.

A Baptist Response

What can one say about Leanne Van Dyk's excellent exposition of Reformed views of the Lord's Supper except "Bravo!"? Hers is the best brief explanation of the subject I have ever read. Most leave Zwingli completely out, as if he were not Reformed! The Zwinglian view of the Lord's Supper is usually treated as the view of Baptists and Pentecostals rather than of Reformed Protestants. I am delighted to know that at least Van Dyk considers it to be part of the Reformed tradition. I have known many Reformed people over the years who regard the Lord's Supper in exactly that way.

The only criticism I have is that the chapter's title, "*The* Reformed View of the Lord's Supper," does not quite fit the content. Van Dyk seems to allow for *three* distinct and legitimately Reformed views of the Lord's Supper. There is, then, no one "Reformed View of the Lord's Supper."

I have no trouble with Zwingli's or Bullinger's interpretations of the Lord's Supper; only Calvin's view confuses me, and it always has. Van Dyk's explanation helps some, but it still seems to me that Calvin wanted to have his cake and eat it too. He wanted the Lord's Supper to be more than a memorial or parallel (with grace); he wanted it to be an efficacious sacrament, a true instrument and channel of God's grace and means of eating the real body and drinking the real blood of the Lord. On the other hand, he wanted to deny the ubiquity of Christ's body and picture Jesus as localized in heaven.

How can he have it both ways? Appeal to the mediating work of the Holy Spirit does not really help. How does the Holy Spirit make the localized body and blood of Christ present in, with and under the sacramental elements of bread and wine? This seems like more than a mystery: it seems like a contradiction. Zwingli and Bullinger were right: the sign and the signified cannot be identical. They were also right that if we are to take the incarnation with utmost seriousness, we must picture Christ's glorified body as a real body localized somewhere and not omnipresent.

The one element of Calvin's view with which I can agree (and remain a good Baptist!) is that there is an intensification of grace in the faithful communal celebration of the Lord's Supper. The present and active grace in that setting, however, is not different in kind from that in any other place or time where two or three are gathered in Jesus' name. Nor is it different in degree from all other active presences of grace. A good gospel sermon can make grace present and active in the lives of hearers. However, the Lord's Supper is irreplaceable; the grace present and active among God's faithful gathered people is special in the sense that this God-ordained ceremony cannot be dispensed with or replaced by something else without losing an important experience of transforming grace. But we can say the same about the preaching of the Word.

A Pentecostal Response

Reading Leanne Van Dyk's careful consideration of the differences within the Reformed family of churches regarding the understanding of the Lord's Supper was very helpful for a theologian coming from another tradition. It is quite remarkable what she mentions in the preface to the essay: "The three early Reformed leaders who formulated distinct Reformed Eucharistic theology were Ulrich Zwingli, Heinrich Bullinger and John Calvin. The clear differences between these three give rise to the observation that differentiation on Lord's Supper theology in the Reformed tradition is much broader than within the Lutheran or Catholic traditions." Van Dyk's way of outlining these three traditions in terms of "memorialism," "parallelism" and "instrumentalism" greatly helps in clarifying a complex and complicated issue. I am sure teachers and students alike, among others, will appreciate this helpful mapping out of Reformed options. At the same time, Van Dyk rightly also points to the many shared convictions among the Reformed churches about this sacrament.

As a Pentecostal, I was intrigued by Van Dyk's highlighting of the central role of the Holy Spirit in Calvin's understanding of the Lord's Supper. According to her, "The prominent role of the Holy Spirit in Calvin's Lord's Supper doctrine is striking. For Calvin, everything depends on the Spirit. Neither sermon nor sacrament will point to Jesus Christ without the action of the Holy Spirit. Calvin says simply that 'they are of no further benefit unless the Holy Spirit accompanies them.'" I am wondering if the same can be said of Zwingli's understanding of the Lord's Supper, and if so, what might be the potential differences between the two. It is striking to me that none of our other writers, Roman Catholic or Baptist or Lutheran, is speaking much about the Spirit's role. There is much talk about Christ, and rightly so; yet a pneumatological orientation would be in keeping with Christian tradition. For a more pronounced pneumatological discussion, we would need a theologian from the Eastern Christian tradition.

Van Dyk's essay bursts with many pregnant ideas about the Lord's Supper, on which she hopefully has opportunities in the future to say more, such as the ethical and pastoral implications. While neither of those features is in any way foreign to Protestant Christianity in general or the Reformed in particular, there is also a recovered interest in such features, along with a revival of sacramental spirituality among churches that have traditionally devoted most attention to Scripture and preaching.

4

THE BAPTIST VIEW

Roger E. Olson

A popular story about Baptists involves a Baptist stranded alone on a desert island. He was there about a year before rescuers finally reached him. As they walked up the beach toward the unkempt castaway, they saw three huts behind him among the trees. "What are those buildings?" asked one of the rescuers. The castaway pointed to the one on the left and replied, "That's my house; I live there." "What are the other ones?" Pointing to the tiny building on the far right, the man said, "That's my church; I worship there." "Then what's the one in the middle?" "Oh, that used to be my church."

Baptists are notoriously diverse: at least fifty-seven varieties exist in the United States alone, and many more can be found in other parts of the world. The largest and perhaps best known among them is the Southern Baptist Convention (SBC), with around sixteen million members in the United States. Its northern counterpart was formerly known as the Northern Baptist Convention but now is the American Baptist Churches USA (ABCUSA). It boasts somewhere between one-and-one-half and two million members. Other Baptist groups in the United States include The Cooperative Baptist Fellowship (a group of moderate to progressive Baptist churches emerging out of the Southern Baptist Convention), the Conservative Baptists of America, the Free Will Baptists (in two or three distinct conventions), the National Baptist Convention (predominantly African American), the Baptist General Conference (formerly Swedish Baptists) and the General Association of Regular Baptist Churches (generally considered fundamentalist).

Baptist diversity is wild. At one extreme end of the spectrum are the Primitive Baptists, who practice foot washing as an ordinance and require other Baptists who join them to undergo new baptism because they consider even other Baptists' baptisms to be "alien immersion." At the other extreme end lie the Spiritual Baptists, composed mostly of immigrants from the Caribbean islands. They practice a kind of séance as part of their worship service.

The point is that there is no "Baptist church"; there are only Baptist churches grouped in conferences or conventions. There are no Baptist bishops comparable to bishops in the Catholic or Episcopal churches; every Baptist church is entirely autonomous and cooperates voluntarily with other Baptist churches for the purposes of missions and education. There is no unifying Baptist creed or confessional statement; Baptist groups have promulgated many Baptist statements of faith, but none are considered binding in any way analogous, for example, to the Westminster Confession of Faith, which is the unifying, binding and authoritative confessional statement of Presbyterians worldwide. Perhaps the best-known Baptist doctrinal statement is the Baptist Faith and Message, first written by Southern Baptists in 1925. The SBC existed for eighty years without any such confessional statement. Since 1925 it has undergone two substantial revisions: 1963 and 2000. Many Southern Baptist congregations make public their disdain for the 2000 revision and declare their allegiance to the 1963 Baptist Faith and Message.

Baptists like to joke that they do not belong to any organized religion; they are Baptists! They hope others will grasp the irony and laugh with them. But this blooming, buzzing confusion of Baptists makes it exceedingly difficult if not impossible to speak about Baptist beliefs as if Baptists agree unanimously about anything. Even identifying a Baptist consensus is challenging. Many have attempted it, but every time they do so, some group of Baptists repudiates the description while claiming to be as truly Baptist as anyone else. Every Baptist group prefers self-description to other-description. Often such self-descriptions are slanted toward what makes that particular group of Baptists distinctive; such descriptions often specialize in reacting to perceived errors among other Baptists and among other Christians.

Probably no single doctrine or practice unites Baptists as much as baptism. Baptists insist on baptizing only persons old enough and willing to confess their faith in Jesus Christ for themselves. They eschew infant baptism even as they sometimes fall into "kiddy baptism"—baptizing children as young as six or seven who are able to give testimony of their conversion to Christ by repentance and faith. Most Baptists reject any sacramental understanding of baptism that would imply a salvific aspect of the ordinance. This is in contrast to Roman Catholics, Lutherans and the Churches of Christ (the latter of which considers adult baptism by immersion necessary for full salvation). The vast majority of Baptists also practice only baptism by complete immersion in water in the name of the Father, Son and Holy Spirit. They regard this baptism as a public act of commitment, declaring a person's death to sin (repentance) and resurrection to new life in Christ (regeneration).

More controversial among Baptists is what to do with persons applying for membership in a Baptist congregation who were baptized as infants and do not want to be "rebaptized" by immersion as an adult (or adolescent) believer. Most Baptists in the United States require such persons to be baptized by immersion upon confession of faith. Some in the United States and in Great Britain, however, have begun to loosen that requirement and accept into full membership persons baptized as infants and/or by sprinkling. This concession to ecumenism has begun to develop and grow especially among American Baptists (ABCUSA) in the last decades of the twentieth century and the first decade of the twenty-first century. Many more-conservative Baptists are horrified by that perceived defection from Baptist tradition.

This brings us to the problem of defining and describing "*the* Baptist view of the Lord's Supper." No such thing exists. There probably is a general consensus among Baptists about what the Lord's Supper *is not* (e.g., a means of grace), but little real consensus exists about what it *is*. All one can do is describe Baptist history with regard to this doctrine and practice and record the exceptions to the rough consensus in a particular time and place. A problem with this historical approach is where to begin the Baptist story. With the early Anabaptists such as the Swiss Brethren in 1525? Or with the first English Baptists, John Smyth and Thomas Helwys in 1610 and 1611, in Holland? Or perhaps, as some would argue, with the organization of Particular Baptists (Calvinists with Puritan leanings) in England in the 1630s or 1640s (pinning down dates in Baptist history is notoriously difficult)? And who speaks for Baptists about this or any other subject? There is no Baptist pope or magisterium of any kind.

In my view the Baptist tradition began with the Anabaptists in Europe in 1525, when Conrad Grebel and Felix Manz, two followers of the Swiss reformer Ulrich Zwingli, defected from the Reformed movement in Zurich and baptized each other upon confession of faith by pouring. The generally recognized first Baptists Smyth and Helwys were in communication and perhaps communion with Anabaptists (Mennonites) in Holland and no doubt adopted their Baptist faith and practice from them. The Mennonites (the largest single group of Anabaptists) never fully embraced these first Baptist congregations for cultural reasons and due to suspicion about their beliefs and motives. Nevertheless, out of this beginning in 1608–1609 in the Netherlands sprang the modern Baptist movement, inspired to a large degree by Anabaptists.[1] I prefer to talk about "baptists" in order to include Anabaptists and Baptists (and perhaps other free-church people) together under a single historical umbrella.[2]

The baptists (with a small "b") have tended to reject Catholic and mainline Protestant interpretations and practices of the Lord's Supper (to say nothing, of course, of the Eastern Orthodox interpretations and practices). The word *sacramentarian* has confusingly been coined by historical theologians to refer to this rejection of sacraments as means of grace. Here, of course, "means of grace" means visible and material objects such as water, bread and wine as conveyers of grace. Baptists do not necessarily reject grace present and active in the ceremonies of baptism and the

---

[1] For the story of the first Baptist congregations and their association with Mennonite Anabaptists in Holland around 1610, see Jason K. Lee, *The Theology of John Smyth: Puritan, Separatist, Baptist, Mennonite* (Macon, Ga.: Mercer University Press, 2003).

[2] I adopt this habit of referring to Anabaptists and Baptists together as "baptists" from Baptist theologian James W. McClendon. See his *Doctrine: Systematic Theology, Volume II* (Nashville: Abingdon Press, 1994).

Lord's Supper. What they have usually rejected is any idea that the grace of God is especially attached to these visible, physical objects or emblems (bread and wine/grape juice) and especially that participants in the Lord's Supper actually eat Christ's body and drink his blood. (Baptists typically interpret John 6:53-56 metaphorically; Jesus was with the disciples when he said people must eat his flesh and drink his blood.) Baptists do insist that God's supernatural presence, power and grace appear in a special way among God's people when they participate in the ordinances (baptists' preferred term for baptism and the Lord's Supper) with genuine faith (including repentance). This "special presence," however, is not different in kind or degree from God's presence in ordinary faith-filled worship and proclamation. "Special" here means simply "distinctive" and not "greater." Baptists also reject any idea of a "real presence" of the body and blood of Christ in, with or under the emblems of bread and wine/grape juice. That does not mean they believe in a "real absence" of the Lord in the Supper, as some critics have alleged. Rather, they regard the emblems as symbols (not "mere symbols," as some have said, but "visible words") of Christ's death and the Communion service as a "memorial meal" that commemorates the same. Baptist folk theology probably has vulgarized these emblems and the Communion service so that they are "mere symbols" and "nothing more than a memorial meal," but baptist theologians have often insisted that the emblems are objects in an event in which Christ is present and active in strengthening participants' faith.

To see if the foregoing description of baptist belief about the Lord's Supper is at least somewhat accurate, it will be helpful to look at some of the more influential baptist statements about the Lord's Supper. One of the first baptist theologians to write about the Lord's Supper was Balthasar Hubmaier (ca. 1480–1528), a Catholic priest turned Radical Reformer who debated with Catholics and Protestants (especially Zwingli) about a variety of issues, including predestination and free will (he believed in the latter) and the sacraments. He was a prolific writer: his collected works fill a hefty volume.[3] His 1527 essay "A Form of the Supper of Christ" expressed his mature thought about the subject. There he set forth

---

[3] H. Wayne Pipkin and John H. Yoder, eds., *Balthasar Hubmaier: Theologian of Anabaptism* (Scottdale, Penn.: Herald Press, 1989).

a definite liturgical form for the celebration of the Lord's Supper for Anabaptist congregations and urged that this ceremony, which he called a "sacrament," should be observed regularly, with sincere self-examination, repentance and faith for the sake of "the communion of the whole heavenly host and the universal Christian church, outside of which there is no salvation."[4] Immediately he continued by cautioning: "Not that here bread and wine are anything other than bread and wine; but according to the memorial and the significant mysteries for the sake of which Christ thus instituted it."[5] Some contemporary baptist theologians have tried to argue that early baptist leaders and thinkers such as Hubmaier believed the Lord's Supper to be a true sacrament in the sense that Christ's real presence is with the elements of bread and wine, and that faith is strengthened through a special grace imparted by them.[6] While Hubmaier and other early baptists did use the term *sacrament* and did believe in a real presence of Christ through the Holy Spirit in the faithful observance of the Lord's Supper by the congregation, they did not consider the elements or emblems of bread and wine to be anything other than bread and wine, and they believed the ceremony itself to be a memorial meal. (I eschew the words *mere* and *only* because they are unnecessary; it is better simply to say that this is what it is; the only negative is that there is no special, supernatural presence of Christ in, with or under the elements or in the ceremony that cannot exist in other places and times.)

Throughout his essay on Christ's Supper, Hubmaier repeatedly refers to its memorial function and denies any special, sacramental presence of the body of Christ. "Bread is bread and wine [is] wine in the Lord's Supper, and not Christ" because "[Christ] ascended into heaven and is sitting at the right hand of God his Father, whence he shall come again to judge the living and the dead."[7] Beginning with Hubmaier, virtually all baptists have believed that Christ's risen, glorified and ascended body resides

---

[4] Ibid., p. 399.

[5] Ibid.

[6] See, for example, several chapters by different baptist theologians with a common purpose (to promote a sacramental understanding of baptism and the Lord's Supper among baptists) in *Baptist Sacramentalism*, ed. Anthony R. Cross and Philip E. Thompson (Carlisle, U.K.: Paternoster Press, 2003).

[7] Pipkin and Yoder, *Hubmaier*, p. 407.

"in heaven" and is not, as Luther claimed, ubiquitous except through the mediation of the Holy Spirit. Thus "Christ cannot be eaten or drunk by us otherwise than spiritually and in faith. So then he cannot be bodily the bread either but rather in the memorial which is held, as he himself and Paul explained."[8] Hubmaier, then, left the door open to a kind of sacramental presence of Christ in the Communion service as a memorial of Christ's death. For him, however, this was Christ's presence through the Holy Spirit to faith and does not involve any special spiritual reality imparted to or by bread and wine.

Menno Simons (1496–1561) was the leading theologian of the Anabaptist movement throughout much of the sixteenth century. His influence on baptist faith and life has been incalculable. Menno's treatise "On the Lord's Supper" sets forth a baptist vision of Communion that almost certainly influenced the first English Baptists as they came into contact with Mennonites in Holland. He rejected any high sacramental understanding of the Lord's Supper while continuing to call it a sacrament. Menno compared it with the Jewish Passover meal and called it a "memorial act."[9] "So," he wrote, "in the Lord's Supper the bread is called the body, and the wine the blood of the Lord: the sign signifies the reality. Not that it actually is the flesh and blood of Christ, for with that He ascended into heaven and sitteth at the right hand of His Father."[10] The purpose of the Lord's Supper is to "commemorate the gracious favors of [Christ's] fervent love."[11]

Like Hubmaier and some later Baptists, Menno did acknowledge a sense of Christ's real presence in the Lord's Supper. For him, Jesus Christ is present with his grace wherever the Supper is celebrated with faith, love and attentiveness.[12] He even affirmed that believers eat Christ in a spiritual sense when they participate in the Lord's Supper, but he distinguished between an "outward eating" and an "inward eating" and limited the Lord's Supper to the latter. By that he meant a mystical union with Christ enhanced by the Supper without any bodily presence of Christ in,

---

[8] Ibid.

[9] Menno, *The Complete Writings of Menno Simons*, trans. Leonard Verduin, ed. J. C. Wenger (Scottdale, Penn.: Herald Press, 1956), p. 143.

[10] Ibid.

[11] Ibid., p. 147.

[12] Ibid., p. 148.

with or under the elements. In general, however, Menno treated the Lord's Supper as a symbolic memorial meal: "It symbolizes Christian peace, unity, brotherly love, and a pious, unblamable life, as has been heard."[13]

Some contemporary baptists who wish to move the baptist churches toward a more sacramental understanding and practice of the Lord's Supper find in Menno and other early baptists a greater appreciation for a real presence of Christ in the Meal. Admittedly, hints of that do exist here and there in these early baptist writings. The overwhelming emphasis, however, is on the Supper as commemoration and as a memorial meal in which Christ is present to faith through the Holy Spirit. If that is sacramental, then so be it. A true, historical baptist understanding of the Lord's Supper may be sacramental in that sense. But it is not so in the sense of an "outward eating" of Christ either spiritually (as in a typical Reformed understanding) or bodily (as in Catholic and Lutheran understandings). Nor is it a sacrament in the sense of a means of grace greater than worship or proclamation.

At this point it will be helpful to turn to some of the most influential baptist statements of faith from the sixteenth to the twentieth centuries to discover what baptists have set forth there about the Lord's Supper. These are supposed to be consensus statements of baptist belief, which baptists have rarely treated as official, binding pronouncements. For example, in most baptist ordination services, deacons and ministers are asked about their faith in relation to the Bible and one or more baptist statements of faith, but they are not asked to swear allegiance to any creed or confessional statement. One of the earliest such baptist confessions of faith is the Ana-baptist Schleitheim Confession of 1527, which called the Lord's Supper "a remembrance of the shed blood of Christ."[14] Another early Anabaptist statement called An Account of Our Religion, Teaching and Faith (Peter Riedemann, 1540) referred to it as "an act of remembrance at which God's children become aware again of the grace which they have received."[15] The Anabaptist Waterlander Confession (Jacob Scheedemaker et al., 1577) said that in the Lord's Supper "Christ's death and bitter suffering

---

[13] Ibid., p. 155.
[14] W. L. Lumpkin, *Baptist Confessions of Faith* (Valley Forge, Penn.: Judson Press, 1959), p. 25.
[15] Ibid., p. 40.

are proclaimed, and all these things are done in commemoration of him."[16] The Anabaptist Dordrecht Confession of 1632 called the Lord's Supper a sacrament but went on to say that its observance is

> to remind us of the benefit of the said death and sufferings of Christ, namely, the redemption and eternal salvation which He purchased thereby, and the great love thus shown to sinful man; whereby we are earnestly exhorted also to love one another—to love our neighbor—to forgive and absolve him—even as Christ has done unto us—and also to endeavor to maintain and keep alive the union and communion which we have with God, and amongst one another; which is thus shown and represented to us by the aforesaid breaking of bread.[17]

These four important early Anabaptist statements of faith say little or nothing about any bodily presence of Christ in the Lord's Supper; they all emphasize the aspects of commemoration and proclamation. The phrase "visible words" well expresses their view of the Lord's Supper. All leave room for a sacramental presence of Jesus Christ to faith in the Supper, as do later baptist confessions of faith, but they do not emphasize any special, supernatural grace conveyed through the ceremony that is different in kind or degree from God's grace to faith everywhere and at all times. Rather, the emphasis is on the spiritual benefit of participation with the believing community in the Lord's Supper through memory and hope.

John Smyth's Short Confession of Faith (1609) refers to the Lord's Supper as a sacrament, but like the Anabaptist confessions he underscores its role in provoking memory of Christ's death in believers. For him, the Lord's Supper "setteth before the eye, witnesseth and signifyeth" the Lord's death.[18] Nowhere did Smyth refer to a real presence of Christ in, with or under the elements either spiritually or bodily. Thomas Helwys's English Declaration at Amsterdam (1611) described the Lord's Supper as "the outward manifestation off [*sic*] the Spiritual communion betwene [sic] Christ and the faithful mutuallie [*sic*], . . . to declare his death until he come."[19] In other words, the communion between Christ and his

---

[16] Ibid., p. 61.
[17] Ibid., pp. 73-74.
[18] Ibid., p. 110.
[19] Ibid., pp. 120-21.

people is there apart from the Lord's Supper, but the Supper symbolizes that communion. Presumably Helwys would allow that by symbolizing spiritual communion with Christ, the Lord's Supper does something to strengthen it; in terms of later philosophy of language, it functions as a "speech act" that not only declares but also enacts.

The General Baptist Orthodox Creed of 1679 contains a lengthy article on the Lord's Supper (chap. 33) and calls it a sacrament. However, the focus is on "remembrance" of Christ's death in the Meal. What is interesting about this baptist statement of faith is its affirmation of a spiritual effect of the Supper on participants by providing "spiritual nourishment."[20] Contemporary baptist sacramentalists have jumped on this and used it to argue that at least some seventeenth-century Baptists did understand the Lord's Supper sacramentally. But that is all it says: "spiritual nourishment." If that is sacramental, so be it. However, most people understand the term *sacramental* as referring to a special conveyance of grace through a physical object such as water, bread or wine. The Baptist Orthodox Creed does not refer to the physical objects as spiritually nourishing in themselves, but to the believing participation in the ceremony of remembrance. The Second London [Baptist] Confession of Faith of 1688 also refers to the Lord's Supper as providing "spiritual nourishment" through a "memorial of that one [Jesus Christ] offering up of himself."[21] The almost-constant theme of these and later baptist confessional statements is that the Lord's Supper is a memorial or commemoration that also has the effect of bringing the believer into encounter and union with Christ through the Holy Spirit when faith is present. There is little or no hint of anything special about the elements beyond their symbolic representation of Christ's death and proclamation of his return.

The New Hampshire Baptist Confession of Faith (1833) refers to the Lord's Supper as having the purpose "to commemorate together the dying love of Christ."[22] The 1869 Revision of the Treatise and the Faith and Practices of the Free Will Baptists repeats those words almost exactly. The 1925 and 1963 Baptist Faith and Message (Southern Baptist) calls

---

[20] Ibid., p. 291.
[21] Ibid., pp. 291-92.
[22] Ibid., p. 366.

the Lord's Supper "a symbolic act of obedience [to] memorialize the death of the Redeemer."[23] The 1943/1944 Confession of Faith of the Alliance of Evangelical-Free Church Congregations (German) refers to it as "remembering the Crucified and hav[ing] fellowship with him."[24]

What does this survey of baptist statements of faith demonstrate? It shows a rough consensus of baptist belief about the Lord's Supper, yet without uniformity. Some of them include language that one can interpret as sacramental in the sense that memorializing Christ's death in this manner has the effect of spiritually nourishing believing participants. None of them, however, talk about the Supper as including a real presence of Christ's body even in the semimystical sense often found in Reformed references to the Lord's Supper. Union with Christ is already always there to faith; participation in the Lord's Supper symbolizes and perhaps strengthens that union in the same way that renewing wedding vows symbolizes and strengthens a marriage.

One of the most influential baptist theologians of the nineteenth and twentieth centuries was Augustus Hopkins Strong (d. 1921), who taught and led Rochester [Baptist] Theological Seminary for many years. His mausoleum sits prominently in the Mount Carmel Cemetery near the graves of Susan B. Anthony and Frederick Douglass. His 1906 *Systematic Theology* was used as the primary text for theology courses in Baptist and other seminaries well into the late twentieth century. There his discussion of the Lord's Supper is lengthy and detailed. It focuses on the symbolism of the bread and wine: "The Lord's Supper sets forth, in general, the death of Christ as the sustaining power of the believer's life."[25] Strong follows this general description with elucidations such as these: "It symbolizes the death of Christ for our sins. . . . It symbolizes the continuous dependence of the believer for all spiritual life upon the one crucified, now living, Savior, to whom he is thus united."[26] Lest anyone misinterpret these statements (and others) as referring to a special grace imparted through the bread and wine, Strong goes on to interpret 1 Corinthians 10:16: "Here 'Is it not a

---

[23] Ibid., pp. 396-97.
[24] Ibid., p. 406.
[25] Augustus Hopkins Strong, *Systematic Theology* (Valley Forge, Penn.: Judson Press, 1974), p. 962.
[26] Ibid., p. 963.

participation?' = 'Does it not symbolize the participation?'" And Matthew 26:26: "'This is my body' = 'This symbolizes my body.'"[27] Finally, Strong put to rest any idea of a sacramental grace conveyed through the Lord's Supper: "The Lord's Supper, like Baptism, is the symbol of a previous state of grace. It has in itself no regenerating and no sanctifying power, but is the symbol by which the relation of the believer to Christ, his sanctifier, is vividly expressed and strongly confirmed."[28]

Strong's explanation of the meaning of the Lord's Supper well summarizes the generally accepted baptist view. Strong was a Northern Baptist, but baptists in the South echo his emphasis. This is confirmed by other baptist authorities such as Monroe E. Dodd of the Southern Baptist Convention, whose 1934 book *Christ's Memorial* is one of the few whole volumes devoted solely to the subject by a baptist author. For him, as for most baptists, the Lord's Supper is the "proclamation of a past act, pronouncement of a present experience, prophecy of a future event."[29] Dodd explicitly denies that the Supper is a sacrament and instead calls it a symbol. He compares it to the Passover feast and calls it "the church's wedding ring."[30] The purpose of this memorial of Christ is "to nourish gratitude and stimulate hope."[31] Nowhere does Dodd mention a real presence of Christ in the Supper that transcends his normal presence in faithful worship.

Another more-recent baptist authority is G. Thomas Holbrooks, president of Rochester Theological Seminary, the oldest existing Baptist seminary in the United States. In his chapter "Communion" in the edited volume *A Baptist's Theology*, he tries to recover what he sees as an early Baptist sacramental understanding of the Lord's Supper, including some sense of Christ's real presence in it. He regards the true root of the baptist tradition as Puritanism and blames the Anabaptists for misleading Baptists about the sacraments (toward sacramentarianism). "Whereas the medieval church had dissolved the mystery in Communion by explaining Christ's presence physically in it, the Anabaptists dissolved the mystery in Communion

---

[27] Ibid.

[28] Ibid., p. 964.

[29] Monroe E. Dodd, *Christ's Memorial* (Nashville: Sunday School Board of the Southern Baptist Convention, 1934), p. 11.

[30] Ibid., p. 80.

[31] Ibid., p. 98.

by explaining Christ's presence totally out of it."[32] In light of some of the sources mentioned and quoted above, this does not seem to be an entirely fair assessment of the Anabaptist view of the Lord's Supper. In any case, according to Holbrooks, the chief culprit in the baptist move away from a sacramental understanding of the Lord's Supper was the Enlightenment, in which "the intellectual and moral emphases prevailed."[33] Baptist views of the Lord's Supper, Holbrooks avers, tended to shift toward the Zwinglian and Anabaptist views (sacramentarianism). Further complicating matters have been revivalism and the emphasis on conversion among baptists in America, which have led to a deemphasis on the sacramental aspect of Communion and an emphasis on its individual and inward side.

Holbrooks appeals to baptist theologian A. T. Robertson, who held and argued for a high sacramental view of Communion. Holbrooks tries to develop a contemporary and historical baptist understanding of Communion that is balanced between its Enlightenment and revivalist denigration on one hand, and on the other hand a high sacramentalism of bodily real presence of Christ and grace automatically conveyed through the bread and wine. His first thesis sounds familiar; it is close to the consensus we have already discovered among baptists about the Lord's Supper: "In Communion the good news of that redemptive action in Jesus Christ is dramatically expressed."[34] This is not far from what Hubmaier, Menno Simons, John Smyth, Thomas Helwys and many other baptist theologians have said over the centuries. But according to Holbrooks, there is a real presence of Christ in the Communion, and it is not a "mere symbol." It is, he says, "a genuine remembrance of God's action in Christ with all its implications."[35] Again, this does not sound very different from earlier sacramentarian baptists. Holbrooks pushes on to elucidate what he sees as a deeper understanding of real divine presence in a memorial symbol. "Remembrance," he points out, is the English translation of *anamnēsis*, which means "to recall or represent the past event in such a way as to make

---

[32] R. Wayne Stacy, ed., *A Baptist's Theology* (Macon, Ga.: Smyth & Helwys, 1999), p. 180.
[33] Ibid., p. 183.
[34] Ibid., p. 186.
[35] Ibid.

it currently operative, to make its power available in the here and now."[36]
He even uses the analogy of a married couple renewing their marriage
vows on an anniversary.

So far Holbrooks's attempt to develop or recover a sacramental understanding of the Lord's Supper seems to fail because in essence it is no
different from the sacramentarian views of the Anabaptists and early
Baptists, who considered the Supper a symbol and memorial in which
commemoration is the main thrust. Next, however, he argues that it is
more than a memorial:

> Communion is more than a bare memorial that calls to remembrance
> something which happened long ago. It is a remembrance that draws the
> fullness of God's past action in Christ into the present moment with power,
> so that believers experience anew God's reconciling love.[37]

Through the Communion service, then, God's people actually experience Christ's presence in their midst. The bread and wine are more than
symbols; they bring about an ontological participation in Christ (1 Cor
10:16-17). They are signs that point to Christ's presence.[38]

> As we take the bread and cup, in our hearts we experience communion
> with Christ and with each other. It is a fellowship meal in the fullest sense.
> Through this Communion we are truly the body of Christ, for as Christ
> makes himself present to us all, he makes us all one in himself.[39]

A question naturally arises for Holbrooks's contemporary baptist
sacramental account of the Lord's Supper: How different is it really from
the essence of that baptist consensus discovered and expressed earlier
here? Some early Anabaptists and Baptists referred to the Lord's Supper
as a sacrament, so that is not new. Many of them also expressed belief in
a real presence of Christ in the celebration of the Lord's Supper while
eschewing belief in a *bodily* presence (even via the Holy Spirit) of Christ
in, with or under the elements. Holbrooks does not seem to think that the
emblems of bread and wine become physical channels of special grace; his

---

[36] Ibid., p. 187.
[37] Ibid.
[38] Ibid., p. 188.
[39] Ibid.

emphasis, like earlier baptists, is on the union with Christ and each other, enhanced by this memorial meal. He calls the bread and wine "signs" rather than "symbols," but the meaning seems to be much the same. Our conclusion here is that what Holbrooks and many other contemporary ecumenical baptists are calling for is actually a return to the baptist theological consensus against vulgarized versions of the Lord's Supper in folk theology (e.g., "merely symbolic").

Another contemporary baptist theologian who writes about the baptist view of the Lord's Supper is John M. Finley in the 1996 edited volume *Defining Baptist Conviction: Guidelines for the Twenty-First Century.* Like Holbrooks, Finley refers to baptism and the Lord's Supper as sacraments without any implication of Christ's bodily presence in the Communion elements or special grace conveyed through them. Unlike Holbrooks, he affirms the baptist tendency to view the Lord's Supper primarily as a memorial meal, whose main function is to recollect and proclaim Christ's death.[40] Communion, he says, is a reenactment of the story of God's love in Christ; it contains a "symbolic presence of Christ in the elements *and* in the believer's spiritual participation with Christ."[41] This is no "mere symbol," however, because of the real spiritual presence of Christ in the elements. One is tempted to think that Finley is a bit confused here. He seems to be mixing uses of *symbol* and *presence.* On the one hand he appeals to Zwingli, who is generally thought to stand behind the baptist view of the Lord's Supper. Against Luther, Zwingli denied any real presence of Christ in the elements and called the Supper a memorial meal. (The early Anabaptists picked up on this and used it to develop their sacramentarian view of the Lord's Supper.) On the other hand he appeals to John Calvin, who understood the Supper as containing and communicating a real presence of the Lord that is more than symbolic. It is spiritual. For Finley, the Supper is "a commemorative meal with depth."[42]

Both Holbrooks and Finley, together with many contemporary ecumenically minded baptist theologians, want to describe the Lord's

---

[40] Charles W. Deweese, ed., *Defining Baptist Convictions: Guidelines for the Twenty-First Century* (Franklin, Tenn.: Providence House Publishers, 1996), p. 113.

[41] Ibid.

[42] Ibid., p. 115.

Supper sacramentally while denying any bodily presence of Christ in the elements or any special grace conveyed by them that is different in kind (or degree?) from grace conveyed through worship and proclamation. At the same time, both (especially Finley) want to hold on to the idea that it is a memorial meal. It is difficult to draw a clear line between their views of the Lord's Supper and the earlier consensus among baptists delineated above. Baptists have never denied Christ's real presence in the memorial meal; what they have denied is Christ's bodily presence in any sense that participants are actually eating Christ's body and drinking his blood. They have wanted to say that Christ is especially, or in a special way, made present by faithful, communal celebration of the Supper without implying that this is different in kind or degree from Christ's presence in any faithful worship of God. They have wanted to say that grace is present and active in the Lord's Supper without implying that it is necessary for salvation or even sanctification.

Finley probably speaks for most baptist theologians (as distinguished from laypeople and pastors) throughout the centuries in his description of what is going on in the Lord's Supper:

> In much the same way as physical nourishment must be taken into one's body in order to sustain physical life, so the reality of Christ must be received and incorporated into the life of the Christian in order to assure spiritual vitality. Most Baptists would be comfortable with such an understanding of Christ's "presence" in the meal and would acknowledge that the proper response to God's gracious act in Christ is *eucharist*, or "to give thanks"—an emphasis of Christ himself.[43]

This is closer to the Reformed view of the Lord's Supper as a sacrament than to the vulgarized version of it as a "mere symbol," a view swimming around in so many baptists' minds. But it is still not quite the Reformed view. Yet even if it is, that shouldn't be a problem. There is no need to exaggerate differences. The point is that most baptists, including revisionists such as Holbrooks and Finley, view Christ's presence in the memorial meal of the Lord's Supper as spiritual but different neither in kind or degree from his presence in worship and proclamation.

---

[43] Ibid., p. 113.

Earlier mention was made of a movement of contemporary baptist revisionist theologians who wish to rediscover what they consider to be an original baptist sacramentalism. Included are Clark Pinnock, Stanley J. Grenz, Michael A. G. Haykin, Curtis W. Freeman and Elizabeth Newman. These baptist theologians' views are expressed in their essays in *Baptist Sacramentalism*. While they do not agree about everything, they do all wish to overcome the popular baptist idea of Christ's real absence in the Communion. Freeman, for example, argues for a "spiritual sacramentalism" very much like the typical Reformed understanding. He appeals to early Anabaptist theologian Pilgram Marpeck and to English Baptist preacher Charles Spurgeon:

> Regarding his physical presence, Christ is in heaven. Regarding his spiritual presence, he is on earth with the fellowship [people] of the Holy Spirit who gather in his name and partake of the bread and wine in faith and love. More such theological reflection is needed to facilitate a move from a theology of real absence to a theology of real presence.[44]

Insofar as these contemporary sacramentalist baptist theologians reject any bodily presence of Christ in the elements of the Supper and any special, sanctifying grace different in kind or degree from proclamation and worship, they are still within the baptist tradition and consensus. Insofar as they wish to express a sense in which Christ is being eaten by participants in the Lord's Supper or in which the grace of God there is different in kind or degree, they are moving away from the conventional baptist understanding toward the Calvinist or Reformed view. This reader finds that somewhat unclear.

What understanding of Christ surrounds the baptist view of the Lord's Supper? One can safely say it is that Christ is bodily in heaven and is not ubiquitous, as in Luther's view (see above). Christ is able to be present and is present wherever faith is expressed in him and he is worshiped in spirit and truth. The Holy Spirit mediates the reality of Jesus Christ to believers in various settings when faith is present. Thus there is no bodily presence of Christ in the Lord's Supper, but there as elsewhere the Holy Spirit, who is the Spirit of Christ, brings Christ into the believers' midst and spiritually

---

[44] Cross and Thompson, *Baptist Sacramentalism*, p. 206.

nourishes them. But this happens through other means as well. The Lord's Supper is one ceremony or observance that accomplishes this. We celebrate it regularly[45] because Christ commanded it and because we now experience Christ in this way through memory and hope.

What understanding of the church surrounds the baptist view of the Lord's Supper? Baptists understand the church as the people of God gathered voluntarily to worship God in the name of Jesus Christ. There is no hierarchy of spiritual authorities. Christ is always present in and among his people when they gather in faith. Thus the Lord's Supper is a way of communing with each other and with Christ; it is a communal event of memory and proclamation that strengthens the unity of the church. There is no special priesthood that officiates; any believer can lead in the Lord's Supper as a priest unto God. The church's central event is the proclamation of the word of God, and in the Lord's Supper "visible words" proclaim Christ's death until he returns. Just as faithful preaching communicates Christ and helps believers commune with him, so the Lord's Supper draws faithful participants closer to Christ and each other. The church is built up by this means as well as by others.

---

[45] The frequency of observance of the Lord's Supper varies greatly among baptists. Most celebrate the ordinance on the first Sunday of each month, but there is no particular reason for that. Many observe communion once quarterly and some (especially in the South) only twice yearly. When I asked my first class of students at Baptist-related Truett Theological Seminary, most of whom come from Southern states, why twice yearly, one said "Because we don't want to be like the Churches of Christ, who observe it every Sunday." Other students agreed. The Baptist church where I hold membership celebrates the Lord's Supper twice monthly or even every other Sunday. The practice varies, apparently without any particular reason.

A Roman Catholic Response

A word of appreciation to Roger Olson for outlining Baptist diversity, giving a positive witness to Baptist faith and helping us with an ecumenical methodology in approaching the Baptist communities.

I live among Southern Baptists and work for a seminary with 10 percent Baptists, only one of whom belongs to the SBC (Southern Baptist Convention). It is a gift for me to be able to read of the multiple streams of Baptist faith and theological witness. Giving our students access to their own tradition is an important task. Self-stereotyping is easy when Baptists are a majority and assertive, and when one group is willing to speak for all. Hence, it is valuable for Baptist and other students to understand various positions in theology and practice, and for the professors to help them understand how Baptist strands have emerged out of the greater Christian tradition, as Olson and others interpret that history.

The emphasis on individual faith, as well as the faith of the celebrating community, and "the faith of the church through the ages" in the mystery of the Lord's Supper—all this is an important witness that Baptists bring to the whole Christian family. Often the rest of us do not hear this positive biblical dimension of Christian witness because of negative polemics that Baptists frequently exhibit toward the majority Christian community, stereotypes recounted in Olson's essay.

It will be helpful for many sacramental Christians to realize that this polemic against their sacramental faith "does not mean [Baptists] believe in a 'real absence' of the Lord in the Supper." Furthermore, Olson's admonitions to Baptists about the desacralizing influences of the Enlightenment and pietism are well taken by all who would be loyal to the christocentric biblical faith, however they may differ on its sacramental expression.

Finally, approaches to visible unity in sacraments and church order are not priorities in most Baptist life. Yet an understanding of one another's approaches to the Lord Supper, moving beyond stereotypes and realizing that all Christians, like Baptists, prefer "self-description to other-description"—this can go a long way toward enabling common evangelism, witness in the world and social action. Most Christians will know what Baptists deny of matters that they consider part of the historic biblical faith. However, such division should not preclude common Christian witness and appropriating those elements of faith in the Lord's Supper that will complement the deficiencies experienced in one's own tradition.

Whether Baptists can learn from other traditions will be their own challenge, but the significance of conversion, personal faith and the gathered community, not to mention the untiring witness to religious freedom—these are the biblical heritage of all Christians, stewarded by the Baptists' communities. The personal relationship of Christians in Christ mirrors the real presence of Christ celebrated in the Supper. It will only be with these human Christian relationships that theological dialogue can be built. The dialogue of trust, love and truth makes authentic ecumenical witness possible.

A LUTHERAN RESPONSE

Roger Olson's essay will prove useful the next time I teach "Religious Bodies in North America." I was stumbling over North American Lutheranism's fairly straightforward right-left divide, with a few minor groups on the sides, when there are fifty-seven kinds of Baptists in the United States alone! I observe that Olson traces the Baptist tradition right back to the rebaptizers of Zwingli's Zurich rather than simply to the English separatists of the last decade of the sixteenth century (a local Mennonite once rebuked me for adopting this genealogy in one of our evening adult education classes!).

Lutherans have an irritating habit, rooted to some extent in laziness, of lumping together all other descendants of the various non-Roman Catholic sixteenth-century "patterns of reformation" under the umbrella category *Reformed*. We take this linguistic route even though the more informed among us know that Calvin and Bucer and the tradition(s) descending from them differ significantly from, say, the Arminians and the Anabaptists. And for our part, we bristle with resentment when Roman Catholics refuse to distinguish the Lutheran wood from the Protestant trees.

And yet, as Luther wrote his last major treatise on the Blessed Sacrament in 1544, he painted all his Protestant adversaries with the same brush, identifying a fundamental sameness among Zwingli, Oecolampadius, Karlstadt and Schwenckfeld (Calvin had not registered on his radar screen, being left to attract the polemical attention of the next generation of Lutherans, led by Joachim Westphal). All of them, says Luther, are united in the main point, which is to deny the Lord's almighty divine word that this sacramental bread *is* his body and this sacramental cup *is* his blood. The nuances between the phalanxes of opponents are and remain secondary. So, while Olson points out that some Baptists would like to inch closer to Calvin and away from Zwingli, I do not find him arguing a position truly distinct from that of Leanne Van Dyk.

If our doctrine is to bind the consciences of Christian people, we must keep our noses in and our eyes on the sacred text, breathed out as it is by the Holy Spirit. Glued as I am to Luther's side (not by his personality but by the text "which is too powerfully present," as he put it in 1524), I find the three "Reformed" contributors united in denying the all-decisive word and deed of the supreme Teacher of Christendom, Christ our enfleshed God. It is as though the Eucharistic text they are expounding runs, "This is *not* my body, this is *not* my blood." I miss an appropriate fear and trembling before the living Torah in human flesh and blood, of whom the Father commanded at the transfiguration, "Listen to him!" Like Luther in his great sacramental writing of 1528, I will take "pure blood with the pope" any day over "mere wine" with those to whom the Reformer referred with an uncomplimentary epithet (*Schwärmer*, lamely rendered as "fanatics"). Why do none of the three descendants of Zwingli deal with Paul's commentary on the words of institution, which simply do not mesh with any of the species of Reformed doctrine that they set forth?

A Reformed Response

The sheer diversity of Baptist beliefs makes it difficult to give a single Reformed response to Baptist views of the Lord's Supper. Roger Olson remarks that the "blooming, buzzing confusion of Baptists makes it exceedingly difficult if not impossible to speak about Baptist beliefs as if Baptists agree unanimously about anything." However, Olson does identify some typical Baptist themes in the Lord's Supper, to which a Reformed theological response is possible.

The themes that Olson surfaces include a rejection of the idea that God's grace in the sacraments is particularly linked with the sacramental elements themselves. The Reformed tradition, especially in its connection to John Calvin, does actually stress the deep link between sacramental grace and the elements of loaf and cup. A Reformed believer would agree with a Baptist believer that God is not by necessity bound to the sacramental elements. But the Reformed believer would say that God does, through promise and covenant, bind God's gracious presence to these elements. The appropriate category for thinking about the connection between grace and sacramental elements, then, is promise.

Another theme in the diverse Baptist tradition is the understanding of the sacrament as a memorial meal. The Reformed perspective would concur with the memorial aspect of the Lord's Supper. In fact, a Reformed believer may well wish to explore further what it means to *remember* as an act of the community, with very rich implications for faith formation.

Sometimes certain positions in the debate over the Lord's Supper refer to a "mere" memorial view. But memory is a faith-filled and faith-formative act of great significance and power. Olson cites a contemporary Baptist theologian, G. Thomas Holbrooks, who affirms the richness of memory recalling "the past event in such a way as to make it currently operative, to make its power available in the here and now." This theme of the importance of the Lord's Table as a place of memorial is a shared conviction among Baptists and Reformed.

A final Baptist theme that emerges in Olson's overview is an affirmation of the Table as a place of God's grace. Yet the grace of the Table is similar to the grace of all worship and preaching. Recognizing the limitations of imagining grace in quantitative terms, there is yet a parity of the workings of God's grace in the Baptist tradition. The Reformed perspective does understand the sacraments as an event of "intensified" grace. There is something unique in the way God graces believers at the Table of the Lord. The grace is "concentrated" because, in the Supper, the Holy Spirit unites us to Christ.

What is so interesting to me, as a Reformed theologian, is the evidence of some increased sacramental exploration among contemporary Baptist thinkers along lines that approach the Reformed affirmations. The volume that Olson refers to, *Baptist Sacramentalism*, opens up new possible convergences between Reformed and Baptist. Differences between these two traditions on questions of baptism can perhaps give even greater urgency to possible similarities on the Lord's Supper. That would signal a happy union, to which our shared faith calls us.

A PENTECOSTAL RESPONSE

I have to confess that before seeing any of the essays, I was most curious about what Roger Olson would write in reflecting on Baptist sacramentology. Only my own assignment, looking at the Pentecostal view of the Lord's Supper, sounds more exotic! Whereas the Catholic writer begins his talk about the Eucharist with an emphasis on the unity of the church, the Baptist counterpart tells a story about the mentality of divisions and separations in his own tradition. What a wonderful way of juxtaposing these two traditions, coming from the two extremes of ecumenical diversity.

Even though diversity characterizes all traditions discussed in this compendium of essays, diversity certainly is a hallmark of the worldwide Baptist movement. Again, only my own church context can "boast" of more massive divisions! There also are so many other similarities between the Baptists and Pentecostals: neither is a "church" in the strict theological-ecclesiological sense, nor do they have one spokesperson or one worldwide structure similar to older churches. Furthermore, as Olson rightly mentions, between laypeople and academic theologians are differences in understanding the Lord's Supper: laypersons seem to take it for granted that the Baptist (as well as the Pentecostal) sacramentology is nonsacramental; yet some theologians in both movements have wondered if a more-sacramental understanding would be in keeping with the heritage of each movement.

Olson strikingly traces the origins of the Baptist movement and hence its sacramental theology as beginning from Radical Reformers such as Balthasar Hubmaier and Anabaptists such as Menno Simons. This helps the essay cover not only the Baptist movement but also much of Anabaptism. It also means that, timewise, the Baptist tradition has as long a theological pedigree as the mainline Reformation churches. Yet, though the Baptist tradition includes a number of ecclesiastical pronouncements in which the topic of the Eucharist comes up, there is nothing like the intentional theological reflection on sacramentology of, say, Catholic and Reformed traditions.

While Olson's essay gives a detailed historical and contemporary survey and assessment of Eucharistic views among the Baptists, I would love to hear more about the christological and ecclesiological ramifications. Olson mentions the latter briefly at the end. Or is it the case that a faithful presentation of the Baptist sacramentology dare not say too much of either Christology or ecclesiology for the simple reason that the movement's emphases have not been there when it comes to the spirituality and theology of the Lord's Supper?

Having read Olson's essay, I also see the editor's wisdom to have both a Pentecostal theologian and a Baptist one write separate essays on the topic of sacramentology. With all our similarities, these two movements differ enough to offer a complementary picture of sacramentology outside older churches.

5

THE PENTECOSTAL VIEW

Veli-Matti Kärkkäinen

We believe in the commemoration and observing of the Lord's supper by the sacred use of the broken bread, a precious type of the Bread of Life, even Jesus Christ, whose body was broken for us; and by the juice of the vine, a blessed type which should ever remind the participant of the shed blood of the Saviour who is the true Vine of which His children are the branches; that this ordinance is as a glorious rainbow that spans the gulf of the years between Calvary and the coming of the Lord, when in the Father's kingdom, He will partake anew with His children; and that the serving and receiving of this blessed sacrament should be ever preceded by the most solemn heart-searching, self-examination, forgiveness and love toward all men, that none partake unworthily and drink condemnation to his own soul.

AIMEE SEMPLE MCPHERSON, *DECLARATION OF FAITH*

INTRODUCTION: PENTECOSTAL SACRAMENTOLOGY— IS THERE ANY?

Indicative of the lack of theological reflection among Pentecostals and of their alignment with the nonsacramental free-church tradition, the entry on the sacraments in *The New International Dictionary of Pentecostal and Charismatic Movements* (2002) is authored by a Roman Catholic theologian[1]—as is the entry on the theology of the church![2] However, there

---

[1] Francis A. Sullivan, "Sacraments," in *The New International Dictionary of Pentecostal and Charismatic Movements,* ed. Stanley M. Burgess and Eduard M. van der Maas, rev. and expanded ed. (Grand Rapids: Zondervan, 2002), pp. 1033-34 [hereafter *NIDPCM*].

[2] Peter D. Hocken, "Church, Theology of," in *NIDPCM,* pp. 544-51.

is a short discussion of the Lord's Supper under the entry "Ordinances, Pentecostal" drafted by a Pentecostal theologian.[3]

Along with most other Christians, Pentecostals celebrate the sacrament of the Lord's Supper and practice water baptism; some Pentecostal movements also practice foot washing as a sacrament or ordinance.[4] While we have to take at face value the statement by Walter J. Hollenweger, a leading theological observer of global Pentecostalism, that "the service of the Lord's Supper is the central point of Pentecostal worship,"[5] we also have to acknowledge that Pentecostals have devoted little attention to developing any kind of constructive theology of sacraments in general or the Lord's Supper in particular. Hollenweger rightly observes that even though "there is no fully developed eucharistic doctrine in the Pentecostal movement, . . . there is a clear and well-developed pattern of eucharistic devotion and practice."[6] At times Pentecostals do not even feel the need to have a discussion of the topic in their doctrinal presentations.[7] More work has been done with regard to water baptism since it has emerged as an issue of contention in the Pentecostal evangelistic and missionary work in relation to members of established churches with a different baptismal practice. At the same time, we should also heed the word of warning from a Pentecostal leader concerning the danger of "run[ning] the risk of removing the importance of these ordinances [the Lord's Supper and water baptism] by deemphasizing their relationship to Christian experience."[8] That danger obviously is real for a movement such as Pentecostalism, loaded with antisacramental sentiment.

To determine the Pentecostal understanding of the Lord's Supper and

---

[3] Harold D. Hunter, "Ordinances, Pentecostal," in *NIDPCM*, pp. 947-49.

[4] I am greatly indebted to my colleague Dr. Cecil M. Robeck, professor of church history and ecumenics at Fuller Theological Seminary, for helping me find a number of key sources on Pentecostal views of the Lord's Supper, sources that otherwise would have been inaccessible to me.

In Nathaniel M. Van Cleave, *The Declaration of Faith*, Foursquare Sunday School Lessons, Teachers, year 2, part 1 (Los Angeles: Foursquare Sunday School Publications, 1949), p. 62.

[5] Walter J. Hollenweger, *The Pentecostals* (London: SCM Press, 1972), p. 385.

[6] Ibid.

[7] E.g., Mauri Vikstén, *Terveen opin pääpiirteitä* (Vantaa, Finland: RV-Kirjat, 1980).

[8] Kermit A. Reneau, "Meaningful Observance of the Church Ordinances," in *Live in the Spirit: A Compendium of Themes on the Spiritual Life as Presented at the Council of Spiritual Life*, ed. Harris Jansen, Elva Hoover and Gary Leggett (Springfield, Mo.: Gospel Publishing House, 1972), p. 173. Quite fittingly Richard Bicknell titles his discussion of sacraments "The Ordinances: The Marginalized Aspects of Pentecostalism," chap. 9 of *Pentecostal Perspectives*, ed. Keith Warrington (Carlisle, U.K.: Paternoster, 1998).

sacraments more widely, I am going to employ three kinds of sources: first, statements of faith and other official doctrinal church pronouncements by Pentecostal bodies; second, the views of representative and widely used doctrinal manuals produced by leading Pentecostal leaders and teachers; and third, the results and insights of the long-standing ecumenical encounter between the Pentecostals and Roman Catholics, started in 1972 and still going on. That dialogue has provided the Pentecostals a wonderful opportunity to formulate their theological understandings in dialogue with an ancient Christian tradition. It is worth noticing that in the ecumenical dialogue between the World Alliance of Reformed Churches and Pentecostals, started in 1996 and still ongoing, no discussion of sacraments in general and the Lord's Supper in particular has taken place.[9] In the final section of my essay, I will also take a brief look at emerging constructive Pentecostal theologies of sacraments and the Lord's Supper, coming from a new generation of academically trained thinkers. While these new views cannot be taken as representative of grassroots Pentecostalism, whether via pastors, leaders or church members, their theological and ecumenical significance cannot be discounted either.

In this essay I am going to focus exclusively on classical Pentecostalism's views and thus exclude the views of the charismatic movements within the established churches, as well as other charismatic views. In the current typology (as adopted, e.g., in *New International Dictionary of Pentecostal and Charismatic Movements*), there are three subcategories to the Pentecostal-charismatic movements. First, there is the category of (classical) Pentecostal denominations such as Assemblies of God, Church of God (Cleveland, TN), or Foursquare Gospel, owing their existence to the famous Azusa Revival; second, charismatic movements, meaning Pentecostal-type spiritual movements within the established churches (the biggest of which is the Roman Catholic Charismatic Renewal); and third, neocharismatic movements, some of the most notable of which are the Vineyard Movement in the United States and Canada, African Initiated (or Independent) Churches, and the china house-church movement, as well as innumerable independent churches and groups all over the world. The charismatic

---

[9]"'Word and Spirit, Church and World': Pentecostal-Reformed Dialogue 1996–2000," posted by the World Alliance of Reformed Churches <www.warc.ch/dt/erl1/20.html>.

movements (about 200 million) and neocharismatics (200-300 million) well outnumber classical Pentecostals (75-125 million).

THE LORD'S SUPPER AS ORDINANCE

While classical theology and mainline churches speak of the Eucharist, Pentecostals prefer the term Lord's Supper or Communion. In keeping with free-church tradition, Pentecostals speak of this rite (and water baptism) in terms of an ordinance, which is defined "as that which is decreed or ordained of God; established rule; a prescribed practice of usage."[10] The reason most Pentecostals prefer the term *ordinance* over *sacrament* is that the latter "seemed to imply a self-contained efficacy, independent of the participant's faith."[11] While acknowledging this common assumption among Pentecostals—which theologically is of course inaccurate in that, unlike classical or contemporary sacramental theology, it juxtaposes faith with the sacramental act in a way that makes them alternatives—Harold D. Hunter, himself a leading Pentecostal theologian, rightly remarks that this is neither a necessary nor warranted conclusion. For him "a sacrament refers to those external rites directed by Scripture and observed by the gathering people of God."[12] If this definition—written in the above-mentioned Pentecostal dictionary and thus representative of global Pentecostal views—is a clue to what Pentecostals understand about sacraments, it is in keeping with the "ordinance" theology as distinct from classical sacramental theology, according to which sacraments bring about what they promise and as such are "effective" means of grace.

Hunter further argues that for Pentecostals *sacrament* is to be understood in a way that he calls "cognitive/symbolic" rather than in the causal way that, in his understanding, is the classical notion: *ex opere operato*. In this Pentecostal understanding, Hunter contends, faith is required for the

---

[10] Ernest Swing Williams, *Systematic Theology*, vol. 3: *Pneumatology, Ecclesiology, Eschatology* (Springfield, Mo.: Gospel Publishing House, 1953), p. 149; Ralph M. Riggs, *We Believe: A Comprehensive Statement of Christian Faith* (Springfield, Mo.: Gospel Publishing House, 1954), p. 54; Guy P. Duffield and Nathaniel M. Van Cleave, *Foundations of Pentecostal Theology* (Los Angeles: L.I.F.E. Bible College, 1983), p. 437.

[11] Hunter, "Ordinances, Pentecostal," p. 947. This is not Hunter's own view but rather his description of a common assumption among Pentecostals.

[12] Ibid.

sacrament to be effective. Emphasizing the importance of the recipient's faith is of course in keeping with the free-church tradition. While Hunter does not explain his use of the terms "cognitive/symbolic" in this context, I take it as a typical nonsacramental Zwinglian and free-church view to be explained in what follows. What is clear is that Pentecostals are wary of speaking of sacraments, either water baptism or the Lord's Supper, in any way that implies "automatic" or "mechanical" or "magical"[13] effects apart from a personal faith response.

A look at Pentecostal statements of faith and doctrinal manuals confirms the assumption that the terminology of ordinance is preferred, implying that celebration of the Lord's Supper is something *ordained* by the Lord and that the faith of the recipient of the sacrament is emphasized: "The external observance of religious rites has no value whatever, unless the devout person discerns and enters into the real spiritual reality of the divine grace which the sacrament typifies. The value of the outward form is that it reminds one of the inward reality."[14]

At times Pentecostal leaders who are well versed in theology and the definitions of theological tradition may define their understanding of the Lord's Supper along the lines of classical formulas such as that of Augustine: "A sacrament is an outward rite instituted by Christ which is typical of an inward grace or experience of grace."[15] In that context the term "sacrament" needs to be understood as emphasizing the significance of "remembrance," which is in keeping with the nonsacramental theology of Pentecostalism.

Pentecostals have only a few rules or guidelines regarding the frequency of administering the ordinance of the Lord's Supper. A good example is the set of guidelines of the Christian Church of North America, a Pentecostal movement, regarding the celebration of the Lord's Supper: "Variety exists both as to elements and serving of Communion. The single chalice is used in some churches while others have adopted the use of multiple glasses for

---

[13] E.g., the Pentecostal–Roman Catholic dialogue's "Final Report: Perspectives on Koinonia," no. 68 (published in *Information Service* 75 [1990]: 179-91) for the phase III (1985-1989); and Michael L. Dusing, "The New Testament Church," in *Systematic Theology: A Pentecostal Perspective*, ed. Stanley M. Horton (Springfield, Mo.: Logion Press, 1994), p. 557.

[14] Van Cleave, *Declaration of Faith*, pp. 62-63.

[15] Ibid., p. 62.

simultaneous participation. Some use wine for beverage, others use grape juice; some leavened bread, others unleavened bread. As in all things Biblical concerning which no clearly defined directive is given, it is felt [that] our Lord grants *liberty of choice*."[16] A general rule of thumb is that it be celebrated monthly, often on the first Sunday of each month.[17] A nonliturgical tradition, Pentecostal churches do not prescribe in detail the way the celebration of the Lord's Supper is supposed to be administered or scheduled; most often it is a rather short part of the worship service. As to the persons qualified to administer the Lord's Supper, it is most often an ordained minister or elder, but rarely are there any binding rules; at times someone else can administer Communion. Participation in the celebration is reserved for only those who have made a conscious decision of faith. Children are not allowed to partake in Communion even though they are present in the service. Dangers of a careless celebration of the Lord's Supper are often mentioned with reference to biblical warnings (1 Cor 11:27-32), and the importance of repentance and humility is emphasized.

Surprisingly to mainline Christians and in contrast to Christian tradition, many (especially American) Pentecostals have refused to partake of fermented wine because of their absolutistic attitude toward consumption of alcohol. Aligning itself with American fundamentalism, white Pentecostal movements from their early days especially decided to use juice instead of wine.[18]

THE PENTECOSTAL UNDERSTANDING OF THE THEOLOGICAL MEANING OF THE LORD'S SUPPER

So, what, then, is the Pentecostal *theological* understanding of the Lord's Supper? It is safe to say—and this is generally acknowledged by Pentecostal theologians—that the theological understanding of most Pentecostals is basically in keeping with the Zwinglian understanding. Take, for example, the *Official Manual with the Doctrines and Discipline of the Church of God in*

---

[16] *Fiftieth Anniversary: Christian Church of North America* (Sharon, Penn.: General Council, Christian Church of North America, 1977), p. 23 (emphasis added).

[17] Ernest S. Williams, *Your Questions . . . Answered by Ernest S. Williams* (Springfield, Mo.: Gospel Publishing House, 1968), p. 47; Aaron M. Wilson, *Basic Bible Truth: A Doctrinal Statement of the Pentecostal Church of God* (Joplin, Mo.: Messenger Publishing House, 1987), p. 134.

[18] See Hunter, "Ordinances, Pentecostal," p. 948.

Christ, a predominantly African American movement, currently the largest North American Pentecostal church that explicitly mentions that the Pentecostal view is Zwinglian.[19] Similarly, the British Elim Pentecostal Richard Bicknell, explains that "the roots of Elim's Eucharistic faith and practice are to be found in the Protestant Reformed Tradition that sprang from [the] Reformation theology and practice of Zwingli and Calvin."[20] The Pentecostal view of the Lord's Supper can thus be rightly called a "memorial" view.[21] This "weak" understanding of the memorial meal is confirmed by the "symbolic" understanding of bread and wine.[22]

How is the presence of Christ understood in this Zwinglian framework? Here two tendencies seem to be in a more or less uneasy, dynamic relationship with each other. On the one hand, in keeping with the memorial nature of the meal, there is a need to reject the kind of "real" presence that both the Roman Catholic and Lutheran traditions affirm. Speaking of the Roman Catholic notion of transubstantiation and the Lutheran view of consubstantiation, the British Elim leader J. Maybin says: "Suffice it to say that we do not hold with either of these doctrines. We believe, according to the Word of God and the experience of millions, that men receive Christ only when they accept Him by faith as their all-sufficient Savior." He also calls the "real presence" view "unscriptural."[23] On the other hand, there is a need to affirm the "spiritual" presence of Christ and the spiritual significance of the celebration of the meal. Therefore, the celebration can also be called a "point of encounter" between believers and Christ or a "divine contact point."[24] But how that is to be affirmed theologically is not usually discussed. A good example is the official statement from the United Pentecostal Church. Speaking of Paul's institution of the breaking of the bread and "fruit of the vine," it says: "There is

---

[19] *Official Manual with the Doctrines and Discipline of the Church of God in Christ*, 1991 ed. (Memphis, Tenn.: Church of God in Christ, Inc., World Headquarters, 1991), p. 77.

[20] Bicknell, "In Memory of Christ's Sacrifice," p. 59.

[21] So, e.g., the Pentecostal Church of Finland teacher Juhani Kuosmanen, *Raamatun opetuksia* (Vantaa, Finland: RV-Kirjat, 1993), p. 138.

[22] So, e.g., *Historia de la Iglesia Pentecostal de Chile*, ed. Carmelo Alvarez, P. Correa, M. Poblete and P. Guell (Santiago de Chile: Ediciones Rehue, 1990), p. 54.

[23] Quoted in Bicknell, "In Memory of Christ's Sacrifice," p. 68.

[24] See further in ibid.

also a spiritual significance and blessing in partaking of the sacrament."[25] This said, there is no further attempt to elucidate the meaning of the "spiritual blessing."

Since Pentecostal theology, including doctrinal theology, is highly biblicist, it is understandable that the teaching on the meaning of the Lord's Supper is often based on leading biblical texts, such as 1 Corinthians 11:23-28. Then Pentecostal theologians explicate themes of remembering Christ's death, proclaiming the benefits of Christ's work and future return, as well as emphasizing the significance of our present communion with the Lord and his church.

One of the few Pentecostal manuals that attempts a theological statement about the presence of Christ in the Lord's Supper seems to be speaking of a "real presence" of Christ, yet at the same time echoing the Zwinglian understanding as well as betraying the typical anti-Catholic prejudices (without mentioning Catholics by name). What is significant about this statement is that it explains the presence of Christ pneumatologically:

> We seek a deeper spiritual reality as a present moment [of] experience. We do not believe superstitiously that the bread and wine actually become the physical body and blood of Christ, nor do we believe that there is any virtue in the physical elements themselves apart from their power as figures to point us to the deeper reality which they typify. We do believe, however, that an act of faith in partaking of the elements results in the real operation of the Spirit in us to strengthen us in the inner man and to heal us in our physical bodies. We, furthermore, believe that the reality which the Lord's Supper signifies is our "daily bread" of which we partake day by day.[26]

Having widely surveyed Pentecostal texts on this topic, I consider this statement the most sophisticated and inclusive "Pentecostal" statement of the theological meaning of the Lord's Supper. While it says more than most Pentecostal statements, at the same time it does not say anything that would be contrary to most, perhaps all, Pentecostals' views.

Surprisingly, though Pentecostals have not usually explained Christ's presence in the Eucharist or its spiritual meaning in terms of the Holy Spirit's

---

[25] *Manual: United Pentecostal Church International Articles of Faith; Constitution* (Hazelwood, Miss.: Headquarters, 1978), p. 23.

[26] Van Cleave, *Declaration of Faith*, p. 67.

work, there are a few occasional statements to that effect in addition to the one cited above. J. Lancaster speaks of the early church's experience of the Lord's Supper in terms of a "'pneumatic condition,' a vivid sense of Christ's presence." Furthermore, Lancaster speaks of the dynamic activity of the Holy Spirit in this context.[27] Speaking of the Pentecostal worship service, David S. Bishop expresses the opinion that the celebration of the Lord's Supper should not be merely an appendage to a service nor unrelated to the theme, and that being a climax of the worship experience, the pneumatic activity should be considered with great care: "Finally, the presence of the Spirit of God is the most important consideration. He should be allowed to hallow all with the manifestation of His glory and grace."[28] How this emphasis is related to the exercise of spiritual gifts, *charisms* (an integral part of the Pentecostal worship experience), unfortunately is not explicated. In general, it is my observation that Pentecostals have not paid much attention to the charismatic element in relation to the sacramental element.

In Pentecostal literature one can also find occasional remarks that apparently embrace the essence of sacramental theology in a way that seems to go beyond the Zwinglian memorial view. According to the Foursquare Church theologian Nathaniel M. Van Cleave, "Every meal could be a sacrament—in remembrance of [Christ]."[29] There are also occasional cases where some Pentecostal leaders seem to be speaking of the significance and spiritual meaning of the Lord's Supper in terms approaching a mystical or mysterious nature:

> The Christian faith holds that man is created in the image of God, and that, through His Spirit, he is able to commune with God. But he [man] has no words adequate to describe what he experiences in these encounters with God, nor to explain the fellowship which he has with Christ and with other Christians. Yet these experiences are so vital and meaningful that he has a compelling desire to share them with others. It is in the act of sharing these deeper experiences that he gives witness to the truth that he is indeed made

---

[27] J. Lancaster, "The Ordinances," in *Pentecostal Doctrine,* ed. P. S. Brewster (published by the Author), pp. 81-82.
[28] David S. Bishop, "The Sacraments in Worship," in *Pentecostal Worship,* ed. Cecil B. Knight (Cleveland, Tenn.: Pathway Press, 1974), pp. 112-13, esp. p. 113.
[29] Van Cleave, *Declaration of Faith,* p. 66.

in the image of God, and that the presence of God in his life is real.[30]

In keeping with the biblical terminology, at times Pentecostals try to describe the meaning of the Lord's Supper in terms of "mystery" *(mystērion)*. According to the Foursquare Church, water baptism and the Lord's Supper are called mysteries "because they typified experiences of grace which were the privilege only of those who belonged to Christ, and whose value could be discerned only by converted persons."[31] While this statement makes sense against the free-church and pietistic understanding of making faith a function of personal commitment, it is hardly in keeping with the biblical or classical Christian usage of the term *mystērion*, which denotes the mysterious nature of the operations of God's grace through the mediation of the means of grace.

THE LORD'S SUPPER AND HEALING

One of the distinctive teachings and practices of the Pentecostal movement is divine healing, which encompasses physical as well as mental restoration of health. Healing for Pentecostals is usually expected through the preaching of the Word of God and prayer for healing; at times, a specific charism of healing is looked on as a means of bringing healing (1 Cor 12:9).

In keeping with ancient Christian tradition in which the Eucharist was depicted as *pharmakon* or medicine,[32] Pentecostals at times envision partaking in the Lord's Supper as a place for healing. The Assemblies of God (USA) Bible teacher Peter Christopher Nelson speaks of the Lord's Supper as "a Healing Ordinance": "If you are sick or afflicted in your body and can discern the healing virtue in the body of our Lord, typified by the bread, you may receive healing and strength for your body as well as for your spiritual nature (1 Cor. 11:30-32)."[33] Obviously, while not intentionally explicating it, Pentecostal piety and church life is open to

---

[30] Raymond M. Pruitt, *Fundamentals of the Faith* (Cleveland, Tenn.: White Wing Publishing House and Press, 1981), p. 364.

[31] Van Cleave, *Declaration of Faith*, p. 62.

[32] See further, Stanley Samuel Harakas, *Health and Medicine in the Eastern Orthodox Tradition* (New York: Crossroad, 1990), p. 91.

[33] Peter Christopher Nelson, *Bible Doctrines: A Series of Studies Based on the Statement of Fundamental Truths as Adopted by the General Council of the Assemblies of God* (Springfield, Mo.: Gospel Publishing House, 1948), p. 68.

the idea of connection between healing and the celebration of the Lord's Supper. Indicative of the lack of sustained theological reflection among Pentecostals is the fact that often the relationship between healing and the celebration of the Lord's Supper is missed completely even when the two discussions follow each other. A good example is the discussion on the Lord's Supper immediately followed by a treatment of divine healing, without either discussion making any reference to the other.[34] The Foursquare Church Sunday school teacher's manual encourages the teachers to carefully remind the students of the "significance of the communion bread and fruit of the vine until it is certain that every true believer discerns clearly the graces of pardon, cleansing, *healing* and keeping that are typified in them."[35] It is not uncommon to hear the promise at the celebration of the Lord's Supper that "there is healing at the table."[36]

This theme was discussed in the Roman Catholic–Pentecostal dialogue. With all their differences in theology and liturgical life, there was an agreement that one of the effects of the Eucharist is healing.[37] While Pentecostals do not speak of "sacraments" in the context of healing, Pentecostal spirituality still considers the Lord's Supper, which commemorates Christ's death, as a healing event. This comes to fore especially in the Pentecostal language of "healing in atonement." In the dialogue with Roman Catholics, a statement in one of the Pentecostal position papers stresses the importance of the idea of "healing in the atonement": "It is a cornerstone of the Pentecostal theology of divine healing that provision was made for the healing of the body through the atoning work of Jesus on the cross. In Isaiah's prophecy of the suffering Savior there are three references to the healing of the body (Is 53:4, 5)."[38] Lutheran charismatics,

---

[34] See Harold L. Bare, *They Call Me Pentecostal* (Cleveland, Tenn.: Pathway Press, 1993), pp. 64-67.

[35] Van Cleave, *Declaration of Faith*, p. 63 (emphasis added).

[36] Bicknell, "In Memory of Christ's Sacrifice," p. 71.

[37] "Final Report of the Dialogue between the Secretariat for Promoting Christian Unity of the Roman Catholic Church and Some Classical Pentecostals," *Information Service* 55 (1984/II-III), §40; see further, Veli-Matti Kärkkäinen, *Spiritus ubi vult spirat: Pneumatology in Roman Catholic-Pentecostal Dialogue (1972–1989)*, Schriften der Luther-Agricola-Gesellschaft 42 (Helsinki, Finland: Luther-Agricola Society, 1998), pp. 281-82.

[38] W. Robert McAlister, "The Ministry of Healing in the Church," *One in Christ* 21 (1985): 47; see further Kärkkäinen, *Spiritus ubi vult spirat*, pp. 397-403.

for example, also regard the Eucharist as an avenue for physical and emotional healing. They expect healing to flow from the presence of Christ in the Eucharist as the healing also can come through intercessory prayer or the gift of healing (charism): "A person may receive faith for healing in connection with receiving the Lord's Supper, and many testify to this."[39]

A leading constructive Pentecostal theologian from Singapore, Simon Chan, has made the following statement, one that is both relevant to this context and that arises out of the matrix of Pentecostal spirituality:

> Prayer for healing of the body, mind and spirit must be a regular part of the church's *liturgical* life. As James has taught us, the sick are to be prayed for and anointed with oil by the *elders* of the church. . . . As a healing and reconciling community the church can then extend its healing ministry to the larger world. . . . To believe in the Spirit-filled church means that the *charismata* operate freely within the life of the church, especially in the eucharistic event when the action of the Spirit is particularized, In short, the holy communion should be the best occasion for prayers of reconciliation and healing to take place.[40]

Interestingly enough, some Pentecostal leaders have noticed that the expectation of healing as part of the celebration of the Lord's Supper pushes the Pentecostal understanding toward sacramentalism.[41] How that is resolved theologically is left open. Instead of seeking resolution, two cautions are offered: Pentecostals should be careful of avoiding any "hint of sacramentalism," and the Supper should not be understood in terms of saving grace.[42]

CHRISTOLOGICAL AND ECCLESIOLOGICAL RAMIFICATIONS

One Pentecostal teaching manual speaks of the meaning of the Lord's Supper in a way critical to this movement's theology and spirituality: "Now, does not this Supper also serve to keep our gospel Christ-centric?"[43] What is highly significant in this statement—which is probably theologi-

---

[39] Larry Christenson, ed., *Welcome Holy Spirit: A Study of Charismatic Renewal in the Lutheran Church* (Minneapolis: Augsburg, 1987), p. 286.

[40] Simon Chan, "Mother Church: Toward a Pentecostal Ecclesiology," *Pneuma: Journal for the Society of Pentecostal Studies* 22, no. 2 (2000): 188 (emphases his).

[41] See Bicknell, "In Memory of Christ's Sacrifice," p. 71.

[42] Ibid.

[43] Van Cleave, *Declaration of Faith*, p. 66.

cally more pregnant than the basic meaning the author intended—is that Pentecostalism, contrary to the judgment of many of its observers, is not primarily a "Spirit-movement," but rather thoroughly christocentric.

The theological and spiritual structure of Pentecostalism is the christocentric "Full Gospel," in which Christ as Christ is depicted in his manifold role of Justifier, Sanctifier, Baptizer with the Spirit, Healer of the Body, and the Soon-Coming King.[44] Therefore, what the above-mentioned manual is saying is totally in keeping with this christocentric view of sacraments: "God's covenant dealings with mankind are through His Son, Jesus, who is the worthy and sufficient center of our gospel."[45] Hence, not only the celebration of the Lord's Supper but also the whole worship experience for Pentecostals is "a Christ-centered worship in the freedom of the Spirit."[46]

The way the South African Pentecostal theologian François P. Möller speaks of the relationship between the Lord's Supper—throughout his extensive discussion he calls it the sacrament—goes beyond typical Pentecostal exposition, yet in my understanding is merely explication of what stands at the heart of the Pentecostal christocentric spirituality. His exposition clearly echoes typical themes of the Roman Catholic and Eastern Orthodox incarnational and cosmic theologies, yet in a way that is not necessarily foreign to a Pentecostal understanding of Christology. Under the section "Holy Communion and the Body of Christ," Möller says that "bread and wine represent his corporeal body, precisely because it comes from the same dust and transience. . . . The bread and wine at the Holy Communion confirms Christ's incarnation, precisely because it indicates his mundane body. At the same time it is representative of the whole material creation with which He identified Himself."[47]

Another novel thing that Möller highlights in his exposition of the Lord's Supper is "The Believer's Experience of the Self-Revelation of Christ during Holy Communion." If Christ is the center of the worship service and of the celebration of the sacrament, then it is understandable that the

---

[44]This is the thesis of the highly influential work of Donald W. Dayton, *Theological Roots of Pentecostalism* (Grand Rapids: Zondervan, 1987).

[45]Van Cleave, *Declaration of Faith*, p. 66.

[46]Bishop, "Sacraments in Worship," p. 101.

[47]François P. Möller, *Kingdom of God, Church and Sacraments*, Words of Light and Life 4 (Hatfield, Pretoria: J. L. van Schaik, 1998), p. 164.

Lord reveals himself to the celebrants. In keeping with the Pentecostal charismatic spirituality, Möller explains that the self-revelation of Christ to his people at the celebration may take various forms, such as a word of knowledge or word of wisdom or come in the form of the healing of the body.[48] As said above, not many Pentecostals have reflected on the relationship between the charismatic and sacramental dimensions. Möller's christologically grounded relating of these two is definitely a pregnant theological theme for Pentecostals and all others.

What about the ecclesiological ramifications of the Lord's Supper for Pentecostals? Although it is questionable whether Pentecostals have a distinctive ecclesiology at all, it is also true that instinctively, without intentional theological reflection, Pentecostals have aligned themselves with the free-church ecclesiological tradition. Hence, for Pentecostals the Eucharist is not constitutive for the being of the church as it is for the Eastern Orthodox and Roman Catholic traditions. And while many Pentecostal denominations have bishops, the episcopacy is not needed for the administration of the sacrament; therefore the Pentecostal ecclesiology is neither sacramental nor episcopal. This topic was widely discussed and debated in the Catholic-Pentecostal dialogue.[49]

That said, the Lord's Supper still plays an important role in Pentecostal church life and spirituality. The Pentecostal position paper in the Catholic dialogue seeks to explicate the christological, soteriological, and ecclesiological meaning of the Lord's Supper by quoting the saying of the Eastern father John of Damascus:

> It is called communion *(koinōnia)*, and rightly so, because through it we have communion with Christ and participation in his flesh and his divinity, and because through it we have communion and are united with one another; for since we partake of one loaf, we all become one body of Christ, and one blood, and members one of another, being made concorporeal with Christ.[50]

---

[48] Ibid., pp. 172-73, esp. subheading on p. 172.

[49] See Kärkkäinen, *Spiritus ubi vult spirat*, esp. pp. 263-89.

[50] John of Damascus *De fide orthodoxa* 4.13 (Patrologia graeca 94:1153), quoted in Miroslav Volf and Peter Kuzmic, "Communio Sanctorum: Toward a Theology of the Church as Fellowship of Persons," Pentecostal position paper for the International Roman Catholic–Pentecostal Dialogue, the Eleventh Dialogue (Riano, Italy, May 21-26, 1985), p. 43 (unpublished dialogue material in

The Pentecostal position paper further underlines the fact that the Lord's Supper is the occasion at which Christians share in the benefits secured for them through the death of Christ and celebrate *koinōnia* with Christ. Only the personal presence of Christ makes fellowship with him at the celebration of the Lord's Supper possible. Because Christians have a personal fellowship with Christ, they can also have personal fellowship with one another (1 Cor 10:17). As such, the Lord's Supper expresses the fundamental equality of all God's people. Also, believers at the Table are not side by side as unrelated individuals, because the Supper is a fellowship *(koinōnia)* meal at which the believers are present as the *people* of God (1 Cor 10:17).

Finally, the Pentecostal position paper helpfully states that all four basic activities of the church (edification, service, witness and worship) come to focus in the celebration of communion. First, the celebration entails mutual edification of the community's members. The self-examination, as a necessary prerequisite for entering communion, concerns not so much the members' direct relation to God as their relation to one another. Second, the Lord's Supper is also an occasion for mutual service: at least in the church's beginnings, at the Supper believers expressed their concern for one another in terms of providing for material and social needs. Third, the celebration is also an evangelistic witness as it proclaims Christ's death and resurrection. And finally, it is above all an act of worship, as the worshiping community looks backward in remembering, and at the same time looks forward in celebration, "as an anticipatory experience of the eschatological messianic banquet, enhanc[ing] our expectant yearning for the completion of salvation in the Kingdom of glory."[51]

The charismatic Roman Catholic theologian Peter D. Hocken, an informed observer of Pentecostalism, summarizes well the role of the sacraments in relation to the charismatic elements and empowerment in Pentecostal ecclesiology:[52]

While Word and sacrament should have a major place in Pentecostal-charismatic church life, this movement poses a radical challenge to the inher-

---

the possession of the author); see also Kärkkäinen, *Spiritus ubi vult spirat,* p. 282.

[51] Volf and Kuzmic, "Communio Sanctorum," pp. 43-47, esp. p. 47.

[52] Hocken, "Church," p. 551.

ited clericalism of both Catholic altar and Protestant pulpit. A Pentecostal-charismatic theology of church . . . can unpack the fuller implications for all aspects of ecclesiology (ordained ministry, Word and sacrament, differentiation of ministries, pastoral authority, marriage and family, evangelism, and nurture) on the basis of all members being indwelt, moved, and filled with the Holy Spirit. Pentecostalism thus takes up a concept dear to the Reformation heritage, the priesthood of all believers, but invests it with more existential content in terms of active deputation to worship and service in ministry.

THEOLOGICAL TASKS AND EMERGING VOICES IN PENTECOSTAL SACRAMENTOLOGY

The discussion of the Pentecostal understanding of the Eucharist[53] has revealed that a number of areas call for theological clarification and constructive work. Fortunately, a new generation of Pentecostal scholars is beginning to tackle many of these issues. In lieu of conclusions and in view of helping the discussion move forward, in this final section I will highlight some of the most pertinent theological challenges and tasks that await Pentecostal constructive theology in light of what I understand is integral to the shape and structure of Pentecostal spirituality and theology. I will do this in dialogue with ecumenical views and at the same time point to some emerging Pentecostal contributions currently underway.

More than a question of terminology, it is appropriate to ask whether talk about *sacraments* and *sacramentology* is in keeping with Pentecostal theology. The previous discussion put forward the objections presented by Pentecostals. Yet some emerging Pentecostal voices are saying, in effect, that nothing in Pentecostal spirituality or theology necessarily makes talk about sacraments problematic. Wesley Scott Biddy argues that the fivefold "Full Gospel" scheme of Pentecostalism, introduced above, leans toward a sacramental understanding in that Spirit baptism, evidenced by speaking in tongues[54] and divine healing, "*explicitly* involve[s] *signs* of God's work

---

[53] In this final section of the essay, instead of the term "Lord's Supper," preferred by most Pentecostals, I use the term "Eucharist" because of its traditional and ecumenical significance.

[54] See Frank D. Macchia, "Tongues as a Sign: Towards a Sacramental Understanding of Pentecostal Experience," *Pneuma: Journal for the Society of Pentecostal Studies* 15, no. 1 (Spring 1993): 61-76; "Sighs Too Deep for Words: Towards a Theology of Glossolalia," *Journal of Pentecostal Theology* 1

in the believer," similar to the "signs" of the Eucharist.[55] To talk about "signs" is of course in keeping with the contemporary Roman Catholic and ecumenical understanding of the sacraments, especially the Eucharist.[56] Amos Yong makes the important point that if Pentecostals believe as they do—based on biblical examples (Acts 8:14-17; 9:17; 19:12; among others)—that the healing power and Holy Spirit's presence can be communicated through physical and material means such as handkerchiefs blessed at healing meetings, then why not through Eucharistic elements?[57] It is yet to be seen whether the terminology of sacraments will establish itself among Pentecostal theologians.

What is the relationship of the Spirit to the Eucharist?[58] While ecumenical theology has in recent years paid a lot of attention to this question,[59] oddly enough—as the previous discussion shows—Pentecostals have only discussed the issue in passing. The Pentecostal theologian Amos Yong suggests that it is time for Pentecostals to begin to construct a pneumatological ecclesiology in which the sacraments, in this case the Lord's Supper, are part of what he calls a Pentecostal liturgy that becomes a "sacrament of the Spirit."[60] This makes it possible for Pentecostals to hold on to both *anamnēsis*, remembrance of Christ's work, and *epiklēsis*, the prayer for the Spirit:

So a pneumatological theology of the liturgy highlights the centrality of

---

(October 1992): 47-73.

[55] Wesley Scott Biddy, "Re-envisioning the Pentecostal Understanding of the Eucharist: An Ecumenical Approach," *Pneuma: Journal for the Society of Pentecostal Studies* 28, no. 2 (Fall 2006): 228-33, esp. p. 230.

[56] See, e.g., Edward Schillebeeckx, *The Eucharist*, trans. N. D. Smith (New York: Sheed & Ward, 1968), p. 97.

[57] Amos Yong, *The Spirit Poured Out on All Flesh: Pentecostalism and the Possibility of Global Theology* (Grand Rapids: Baker Academic, 2005), p. 163.

[58] For some constructive reflections, see Veli-Matti Kärkkäinen, "The Spirit and the Lord's Supper," in *Toward a Pneumatological Theology: Pentecostal and Ecumenical Perspectives on Ecclesiology, Soteriology, and Theology of Mission*, ed. Amos Yong (Lanham, Md.: University Press of America, 2002), pp. 135-46.

[59] See, e.g., Wolfhart Pannenberg, *Systematic Theology*, trans. Geoffrey W. Bromiley, vol. 3 (Grand Rapids: Eerdmans, 1998), pp. 283-336, esp. pp. 320-24.

[60] Yong, *The Spirit Poured Out*, pp. 160, 166. See also the significant contribution of Chan, "Mother Church," pp. 177-208; Frank Macchia, *Baptized in the Spirit: A Global Pentecostal Theology* (Grand Rapids: Zondervan, 2005), chap. 5, "Signs of Grace in a Graceless World: Towards a Spirit-Baptized Ecclesiology."

the working of the Spirit in the fellowship of the meal. In this case, the invocation *(epiklēsis)* of the Spirit becomes essential to the church's memory
(anamnēsis) of Christ, both in the sense of enabling the recollection of
the historical Jesus in the present remembering of the body of Christ
and in the sense of making present the living Christ in the "membered"
elements of the bread and cup and in the "members" of the congregation as the living body of Christ. As such, the Lord's Supper becomes a
sacramental rite . . . that transforms the worshiping community through
word and Spirit.[61]

A corollary question is whether Pentecostalism contains any resources
to make a more robust connection between the charisms and the Eucharist. The Orthodox theologian John Zizioulas makes the important
observation that in the primitive Pauline churches charismatic manifestations took place during the Eucharistic gatherings (cf. 1 Cor 11–14)[62] as
well as ordination to the ministry, the latter of which was understood as
the outpouring of the Spirit of God.[63] This is indeed a theologically pregnant idea for Pentecostals; while not unknown to Pentecostal spirituality
and worship life—as a visit to a typical worship service would testify—
neither has it been made a theological theme even though it stands at the
heart of Pentecostal experience.

There is yet another pneumatological theme that should interest
Pentecostals: that has to do with "discernment." How do Pentecostals
understand the Pauline exhortation about "discerning the body" (1 Cor
11:29)? As far as I can tell from the literature, it has been understood
exclusively along the canons of older exegesis in terms of moral lapses
and failures. Although there is no reason to reject this aspect, contemporary exegesis argues that what Paul had in mind was discerning the
unity of the body of Christ, meaning the church. What Paul had in
mind was not the unworthiness of the celebrants because of their failure

---

[61] Yong, *The Spirit Poured Out,* pp. 162-63.

[62] John D. Zizioulas, *Being as Communion: Studies in Personhood and the Church* (Crestwood, N.Y.:
St. Vladimir's Press, 1985), p. 193. At the same time I cannot accept Zizioulas's opinion that
charismatic manifestations appeared *exclusively* in Eucharistic gatherings, although it is highly
significant that the only two Eucharistic texts we have from Paul come to the fore amid his teaching and warning concerning charismata.

[63] Ibid.

in their private Christian walks, but breaches in the fellowship.[64]

This question is integrally related to the ecumenically thorny question of the connection between the Lord's Supper and the unity of the church. This theme was also extensively discussed in the Roman Catholic–Pentecostal dialogue, but no unanimity was reached.[65] Though Pentecostals wholeheartedly affirm the "spiritual unity" of all believers, they have not done much work in relating that affirmation to either sacraments nor to visible unity. That is one of the many tasks awaiting the new generation of theologians in this dynamic movement.

---

[64] For a balanced discussion, see Gordon D. Fee, *The First Epistle to the Corinthians*, NICNT (Grand Rapids: Eerdmans, 1987), pp. 558ff. Cf. Pannenberg, *Systematic Theology*, 3:326ff.

[65] See Kärkkäinen, *Spiritus ubi vult spirat*, pp. 311-23; for a promising constructive Pentecostal ecclesiology that takes the unity aspect of sacraments seriously, see Yong, *The Spirit Poured Out*, pp. 134-39.

A Roman Catholic Response

A word of appreciation to Veli-Matti Kärkkäinen for emphasizing the pneumatological dimension of Eucharistic faith in the sacrament, pointing out methodologies for mutual understanding, and introducing us to theological developments within Pentecostalism.

The Pentecostal churches, like the Reformed and Orthodox, have a more developed experience of the Holy Spirit active in worship, including the Lord's Supper, than was the recorded experience of the sixteenth century. Therefore, attending to the work of the Holy Spirit, to the healing dimension (as does Stephenson) and to the contribution of the community of the Lord's Table to Christian discernment—these are learnings from which all Christians can benefit by listening to one another and attending to the Pentecostal witness. The fact that Pentecostalism "poses a radical challenge to the inherited clericalism of both Catholic altar and Protestant pulpit" is a welcome contribution, though history has shown the limitations of charismatic, entrepreneurial leadership as well.

Kärkkäinen gives a positive view of the christocentric character, the diversity and the irenic potential of Pentecostalism—insights often unavailable to those whose only experience is the polemical and separatist repudiation of fellow Christians in many parts of the world. Yet his essay does report some stereotypes.

Direct dialogue is essential for us to understand that Pentecostal views of the Lord's Supper are rooted not only in the Renaissance, with the rationalistic reductionism of a Zwinglian view, but also in certain biblical claims. Furthermore, it is not enough to read Pentecostal scholarship written by the classically trained. It is also essential to experience Pentecostal worship and to speak to the untutored believer about their positive experience of Christ in the Supper.

Finally, it is helpful to see the intellectual tradition of Pentecostal scholars, who are making accessible to the academic theological community a variety of approaches to Pentecostal worship, understanding of the faith and sacramental/ordinance practice.

There is also a Wesleyan, sacramental strain to the Pentecostal heritage as well as Zwinglian memorialism, which has a different interpretation of the Pauline and Johannine witness. Kärkkäinen's citation of Biddy is a useful resource for exploring this heritage. In Chile, for example, five Pentecostal churches have been able to agree on common baptismal recognition with historic Protestant, Catholic and Orthodox sacramental churches (www.iglesia.cl/).

Pentecostalism is celebrating its first centenary in the Christian family, begun as a movement, developing into classical Pentecostal churches. Now the movement is embodied in sacramental churches of the classical traditions, nonsacramental and sacramental classical Pentecostal churches, and a host of independent communities.

The dialogue on the Lord's Supper has been slow for multiple reasons, many of which Kärkkäinen documents well for us. Therefore we can be grateful for what we all may learn from the Pentecostal encounter, and what the emerging Pentecostal theological community may learn from the other churches in their centuries of faithful testimony to Scripture and its witness to the Lord's Supper.

A LUTHERAN RESPONSE

For much of his essay, which afforded me my first encounter with Pentecostal theology, Veli-Matti Kärkkäinen struck me as saying nothing different from the Reformed and Baptist contributors to this volume. My interest perked up, though, when he mentioned how some Pentecostals are wont to affirm, "There is healing at the Table." Yes, when the Blessed Sacrament is legitimately and validly celebrated, the embodied Christ bestows a full healing of body and soul through the gift of his body given and blood shed. While full in principle, this (eschatological) healing is usually largely hidden in fact, though real indications of healing may appear in soul and body, according to the Lord's will. But I ask Kärkkäinen how Christians should expect healing from an empty Table rather than from the altar on which the Lamb of God takes his throne in his body and blood? Why not accept the Lord's word and the apostle's testimony that the Table is full, that the throne has a king seated on it?

My parting response to Van Dyk, Olson and Kärkkäinen is to recall a "prophecy" spoken toward the end of his life by Wilhelm Löhe (1808–1872), who combined Lutheran orthodoxy and liturgical zeal with a "charismatic" dimension that left many of his coreligionists distinctly uncomfortable. As he gazed into the future, Löhe saw a coming together and sacramental sharing of believing, "evangelical" Protestantism (a grouping that would surely include not only the Reformed in both senses of the word, but also evangelical Anglicans and the spiritual descendants of Philipp Melanchthon) rendered possible by taking a live-and-let-live attitude to the essence of Holy Communion. Notwithstanding Löhe's deep love for many Reformed Christians and his appreciation of their witness and work, he saw this "broad and wide stream" countered by a "small and narrow stream" of Lutherans united in a unanimous understanding of the miraculous effects of the Eucharistic words of Jesus, the chief Consecrator at Christendom's altars. I respectfully remain at Luther's side in Wittenberg and at Löhe's in the Bavarian village of Neuendettelsau (which his ministry put on the map) not out of hero worship but because they both strike me as kneeling in rapt adoration at Jesus' feet in the upper room.

And yet we all have one Lord, who alone can preserve and unite his still-squabbling flock(s). Till we all agree which Supper he actually founded, though, here below we cannot partake of the same bread and the same cup.

A Reformed Response

The Pentecostal tradition is fascinating to a Reformed Christian. This is because many of the Pentecostal emphases are familiar to the Reformed tradition. These features include the spiritual experience of the Christian, the necessity of faith as a receiver of grace and the central importance of the Holy Spirit. Because all of these are affirmations of the Reformed tradition as well, the possibility for ecumenical dialogue and mutual instruction is high.

For example, the 1949 Pentecostal Declaration of Faith states that the Spirit is the dynamic divine agent in the sacrament and that the "real operation of the Spirit in us to strengthen us." A Reformed Christian can readily affirm that all this is at the heart of the Lord's Supper. However, as Veli-Matti Kärkkäinen observes, the explicit reference to the power of the Holy Spirit in the Lord's Supper is actually quite infrequent. The more typical focus is on the believer's faith and on the promise signaled by the sacramental ordinance. The tendency to refer to the Lord's Supper (or baptism) as an "ordinance" itself signals a deep difference in the understanding of God's initiative in the sacraments. The differences between the two traditions are in some respects rather deep.

Yet some of the emphases of the Pentecostal tradition have the potential of real insight for Reformed Christians. The healing aspect of the Lord's Supper in the Pentecostal tradition is an important implication in the Reformed understanding of the Lord's Table as God's gift for God's people, a gift that comes from the spring of God's own care and compassion for a people wounded and weak. In the Pentecostal tradition, the theme of healing is congruent with the Reformed understanding of the Supper as a source of nourishment and strength.

A key insight of Kärkkäinen's description of Pentecostalism's relatively undeveloped theology of the Lord's Supper is the observation that Pentecostalism's ecclesiology is equally undeveloped. The Pentecostal theological efforts that he points to, as well as the ecumenical dialogue, will begin to produce constructive theologies of church and sacrament.

The Reformed response to a Pentecostal understanding of the Lord's Supper, then, is an encouragement to "live into" the full implications of the Holy Spirit as bringing God's gracious presence to us in the loaf and the cup. Kärkkäinen points to several hopeful efforts in the Pentecostal theological conversation, including an understanding of physical and material means as channels of God's grace, an exploration of the liturgy as a means of the Spirit's work, and the Lord's Supper as a locus for charismatic gifts. These are topics unique to the Pentecostal tradition, yet they are fruitful for ecumenical dialogue and instruction, including among Reformed believers.

A Baptist Response

As a former Pentecostal, I read Veli-Matti Kärkkäinen's chapter with great interest. When I first saw that this book would include both the Baptist view of the Lord's Supper and the Pentecostal view, I was surprised and expressed concern about whether there is any difference between them. My transition from Pentecostalism (the first half of my life) to Baptist (the second half of my life) did not seem to include any change in belief about or practice of the Lord's Supper.

Both Baptists and Pentecostals (along with many other free-church traditions) hold to a generally Zwinglian view of the Lord's Supper. Kärkkäinen acknowledges as much, but he strives to demonstrate that at least some, if not most, Pentecostals go beyond that to a near-sacramental understanding of the celebration. In my chapter on the Baptist view, I discuss several recent attempts by Baptists to close the gap between the traditional Baptist view and a more-sacramental belief similar to the prevailing Reformed view. Kärkkäinen does somewhat the same with Pentecostals and the Lord's Supper.

I am most impressed with his discussion of the Pentecostal interpretation of the Lord's Supper having efficacy for physical healing. That I can remember from my Pentecostal days (I first studied theology at a Pentecostal college). Even then I remember thinking that there is a problem with such a belief. It stems from the basic Pentecostal doctrine that the atonement of Christ provides for physical healing. Then and now I have wondered if that doctrine might lead someone to doubt their salvation if healing is not forthcoming from prayers of faith. After all, if the atonement unconditionally secures salvation for everyone who repents and has faith, then surely the same would be true of physical healing. Now look backward from the perspective of a Pentecostal who has repented and exercised faith in Christ for salvation but is not being healed in spite of many prayers. Perhaps such a person's salvation was not real.

I have personally known of several Pentecostals who have struggled with doubt about their salvation because of ongoing physical illness, in spite of faithful praying. One was a Church of God minister who suffered from blood clots. He died of a pulmonary embolism while doubting his salvation because he was not healed.

That was one reason I left the Pentecostal communion behind to become a Baptist. The only change in my belief about and practice of the Lord's Supper was with regard to the ordinance's efficacy for healing. Although God can and sometimes does heal people, there is no guarantee of it secured by the atonement. And the Lord's Supper is no more efficacious for healing than a prayer. Scripture even instructs us to call the elders to pray for the sick. It does not say anything about physical healing stemming from the Lord's Supper.

Nevertheless, in spite of this difference, I see little other difference between the Baptist and Pentecostal views of the Lord's Supper. Both can lend themselves to semisacramental interpretations insofar as Christ is believed to be personally present in a special way as the church celebrates the ordinance. Neither would be true to its roots if it leaned too far toward sacramentalism by regarding Christ as bodily present and eaten together with the bread and wine (juice). I urge Pentecostals and Baptists and other free-church Protestants to hold to their traditional understanding of the Lord's Supper as symbolic without reducing it to "mere symbolism." A real symbol participates in the reality it represents without becoming that reality. A gap always remains between symbol and reality, but it does not need to be a fixed gulf.

CONCLUSION

In a fascinating study of an ancient Roman church—*The Geometry of Love*—Margaret Visser weaves a wonderful series of theological reflections into her comments and observations about the history, architecture and art of what she calls an "ordinary church." And when she pauses to comment on the Lord's Supper, she writes:

> The Eucharist, also known as Communion, is believed to unite Christ and Christians. Each of the people present at the ceremony eats the consecrated bread, and may also drink the wine: in sharing it, many become one. In order to make this possible, however, the bread must first be broken: the one becomes the many.[1]

Her aptly chosen words and observation are a keen reminder of Christ's clear intentions at the Last Supper—that in and through his death and resurrection, Christ himself would not merely unite his disciples to himself, but also to one another. There is no doubt that the Lord's Supper is meant to demonstrate and indeed further Christ's intentions—drawing us not only to himself but also to our sisters and brothers in Christ.

This is to be the Table that unites the faithful. But as patently obvious, the Table that was meant to unite has for so many centuries been a Table of division and separation.

---

[1]Margaret Visser, *The Geometry of Love: Space, Time, Mystery, and Meaning in an Ordinary Church* (New York: North Point Press, 2000), p. 83.

Yet this is not something about which we should become either melodramatic or cynical. Rather, it should do what we trust this collection of essays does: urge us to think deeply and critically about the meaning of the Lord's Supper, but to do so in dialogue and conversation with those whose background, theological perspective and practice is, perhaps, quite different from our own.

And we will differ; most notably on the meaning of the words that are so central to our understanding of the Lord's Supper—"This is my body"—and the implications of this extraordinary declaration for the life of the church. But in our differences may we not leave the table or the conversation or give up our own resolve to learn as we listen to others.

In many respects this is the genius of the document mentioned in the introduction, *Baptist, Eucharist and Ministry (BEM)*. It was intended to foster common understanding through focused conversation around points of agreement and even open disagreement, where this is called for. Nothing is gained by minimizing differences when and if these are matters of substance—when they reflect, for example, a crucial point of understanding regarding Christ, the nature of the church or the character of the Christian life. Yet what *BEM* provides is a benchmark of the fifty years of conversation leading up to the 1982 Lima acceptance of this document and then a basis for ongoing exchanges that now must reference this work.

As recognized in the introduction, *BEM* rightly insists that our understanding and practice of the Lord's Supper must be trinitarian: this is foundational. While our understanding of the Lord's Supper will always be necessarily deeply shaped by our Christology and especially by our understanding of the incarnation of the Christ, it is always about the Christ who is one with the Father and the Spirit. The great danger of some traditions is a kind of docetic Christomonism—the encounter with a Christ who has no seeming reference to the Trinity (or to Christ's embodiment).

Then also, as mentioned above, *BEM* stresses that this is the holy meal of the church, the gathered people of God. It is about our encounter both with Christ himself, yet also with one another. Can it not indeed be said that the Lord's Supper marks the church as the church more than any other single activity or event? That without the Lord's Supper, the gathering is really nothing but a religious club? The Lord's Supper is what demarcates our common life as precisely being the body of Christ, the people of God and the fellowship of the Spirit.

We also must affirm the way in which *BEM* calls all Christians to see in the celebration of the Lord's Supper an act of anticipation and thus of the renewal of our hope. In the encounter with the risen Christ described in Luke 24, we read that the two disciples who, at first unwittingly, meet with Christ refer to him as "powerful in word and deed" (Lk 24:19 NIV). And rightly so; they have been thoroughly impressed with the capacity of Christ to bring healing, justice and peace. But then they have been set back by the horror of the cross and now, deeply disappointed, they exclaim: "But we had hoped that he was the one to redeem Israel" (Lk 24:21).

"We had hoped!" they say. And indeed, in diverse ways we often hear of Christians who "had hoped" in Christ Jesus but for whom now there is a growing and persistent lack of hope. Cynicism seems to be the growing disease of the church, as is so apparent for many who are in religious leadership. They see it and hear it often: cynicism about marriage and family and the possibilities of grace; cynicism about the church, particularly for those who have experienced the pain of political battles and deep church conflict; cynicism about the possibilities that the church can be, as one, an authentic witness to the kingdom in the world.

The two disciples on the road to Emmaus declare, "We had hoped," and in response Jesus does two things: he explicates for them the story of redemption, the story of the cross, and then he meets them in the breaking of the bread. From the moment of despair, Jesus takes the disciples to the Word and then to the Table.

At the Lord's Supper, we do look back, remembering the once-for-all gift of salvation in Christ Jesus. And in this meal we are conscious of present realities—the faith community gathered in communion with the risen Lord. But it is vital that we also remember that the Lord's Supper is an act of anticipation. It is but a foretaste of a meal that is yet to come, when heaven and earth will be one and when justice and peace will embrace. In times of despair and disillusionment, this meal is God's unique gift through which we remember that evil and darkness do not have the last word.

We are reminded not as an exercise of intellect, though it certainly is a thoughtful and theologically informed participation. Rather, we present our bodies, within and as part of the body of Christ, and we are re-membered. We are increasingly made one with Christ as we abide in him and he abides in us, and we are made one with one another in the fellowship of the Spirit. And in this event, in the practice of the Lord's Supper, we surely know that evil does not have the last word. Not just evil but also even legitimate differences, yea indeed, our substantial differences of opinion about the Lord's Supper—these are not the last word.

FOR FURTHER READING

The following bibliography and recommended further reading include annotations from the contributors.

ROMAN CATHOLIC PERSPECTIVES

Benedict XVI. *Sacramentum Caritatis*, 2007. www.vatican.va/holy_
father/benedict_xvi/apost_exhortations/documents/hf_ben-xvi_
exh_20070222_sacramentum-caritatis_en.html.

> While this text bears the authorship of the current Pope, it summarizes the results of a 2005 worldwide synod of bishops in Rome, called by Pope John Paul II. Therefore, it is a very good barometer of current vision and concerns of the pastoral leadership of the global Catholic Church. It is a stock-taking of the liturgical reforms initiated in the Second Vatican Council (1962–1965). It contains links to other important Catholic documents.

Irwin, Kevin. *Models of the Eucharist*. New York: Paulist Press, 2005.

> An important American Catholic theological, spiritual and pastoral contribution to the understanding of the Lord's Supper for the serious theological reader.

Kasper, Walter. *Sacrament of Unity: The Eucharist and the Church*. New York: Crossroad Publishing, 2004.

> A series of essays by a prominent Catholic German theologian, now a Roman Cardinal with responsibility for leadership in the Church's mission of promoting the unity of Christians. These essays are theologically

informed pastoral messages for the people of his diocese in Germany.

Osborne, Kenan. *Community, Eucharist, and Spirituality*. Liguori, Mo.: Liguori Press, 2007.

A contemporary, biblically and historically grounded, pastorally oriented overview of the Lord's Supper for present-day Catholic life and understanding.

Power, David. *The Sacrifice We Offer: The Tridentine Dogma and Its Reinterpretation*. New York: Crossroad, 1987.

An important American Catholic theological, spiritual and pastoral contribution to the understanding of the Lord's Supper for the serious theological reader.

Ratzinger, Joseph (Benedict XVI). *God Is Near Us: The Eucharist, the Heart of Life*. San Francisco: Ignatius Press, 2003.

A solid theological grounding for traditional Catholic devotion, practice and teaching on the Lord's Supper and Eucharistic piety. This is a collection of his preaching and essays before 2003.

Thurian, Max, ed. *Churches Respond to BEM: Official Responses to the "Baptism, Eucharist and Ministry" Text*, vols. 1-6. Geneva: World Council of Churches, 1986–1988.

This series of texts includes the official Roman Catholic response to the World Council's *Baptism, Eucharist and Ministry* (as well as those of the Lutheran Church–Missouri Synod, the Reformed Church in America, numerous Baptist and other church responses), which along with the response to the Anglican Roman Catholic International Commission's *Final Report*, reflect the highest level of Catholic theological concerns about agreement on the Lord's Supper. This text is twenty years old, so that subsequent dialogue will also be of interest to the serious student (<www.prounione.urbe.it/dia-int/e_dialogues.html>, <www.usccb.org/seia/agreed.shtml>)

LUTHERAN PERSPECTIVES

The Book of Concord.

Nonspecialists may wish to consult the attractive edition of the Missouri Synod's English translation of 1917 found in Paul T. McCain, ed., *Concordia: The Lutheran Confessions; A Reader's Edition of the Book of*

Concord, 2nd ed. St Louis: Concordia Publishing House, 2006.

Braaten, Carl E., and Robert W. Jenson, eds. *Christian Dogmatics*, 2 vols. Philadelphia: Fortress Press, 1984. 2:337-66.

> For a Lutheran perspective differing from that found in this book.

Hardt, Tom G. A. *The Sacrament of the Altar* (available on the Internet <users.aol.com/SemperRef> as a condensation of this author's *Venerabilis et adorabilis Eucharistia: en Studie i den lutherska nattvardsläran under 1500-talet*. Uppsala, Sweden: Ljungbergs Boktryckeri, 1971.

> This magisterial work also exists in a German translation published in 1988 by Vanderhoeck & Ruprecht, Göttingen.

Luther, Martin. *Luther's Works*, vols. 35-38. Philadelphia: Fortress Press, 1970–1971.

> Referenced in the body of my essay as AE (=American Edition) followed by volume number. My essay is no more than an extended footnote to the two works included in AE 37 (*That These Words of Christ, "This Is My Body," etc., Still Stand Firm Against The Fanatics*, 1527; *Confession Concerning Christ's Supper*, 1528). According to the Formula of Concord (Solid Declaration VIII, 3), these and other works of the Reformer are not just Luther's private opinion, but belong to "his doctrinal and polemical writings concerning the Holy Supper, to which we herewith publicly profess our allegiance."

Sasse, Hermann. *This Is My Body: Luther's Contention for the Real Presence in the Sacrament of the Altar*. Adelaide, Australia: Lutheran Publishing House, 1977.

———. "Church and Lord's Supper: An Essay on the Understanding of the Sacrament of the Altar" (1938), in *The Lonely Way: Selected Essays and Letters by Hermann Sasse*, 2 vols., 1:369-429. St Louis: Concordia Publishing House, 2002.

Stephenson, John R. *The Lord's Supper*. Confessional Lutheran Dogmatics, vol. XIII. St Louis: The Luther Academy, 2003.

REFORMED PERSPECTIVES

Calvin, John. *Institutes of the Christian Religion* 4.17.1. Edited by John T. McNeill and translated by Ford Lewis Battles. Philadelphia: Westminster Press, 1960.

This classic chapter in Book 4 of the *Institutes* is necessary for anyone who wishes to understand the Reformed tradition on the Lord's Supper. All the expansive affirmations of John Calvin are here, including the believer's union with Christ, the nourishment of the Table and the fatherly care of God in providing the Communion feast.

Nevin, John Williamson. *The Mystical Presence: A Vindication of the Reformed or Calvinistic Doctrine of the Holy Eucharist.* Philadelphia: S. R. Fischer, 1867.

The unabashedly catholic stream of the Mercersberg theology is seen in this classic text from the late nineteenth century. John Nevin's Lord's Supper theology is not the "majority report" in the Reformed tradition, but it has important links to broader Christian traditions and yet presents a clear Reformed accent.

Vander Zee, Leonard. *Christ, Baptism and the Lord's Supper: Recovering the Sacraments for Evangelical Worship.* Downers Grove, Ill.: InterVarsity Press, 2004.

This book, written by an experienced congregational pastor in the Reformed tradition, makes the claim that the sacraments are a vital part of Christian worship and that the congregation's formation in the faith is nurtured in faithful celebration of the sacraments. This book would be helpful in a number of settings, including adult study groups and worship committee meetings.

Welker, Michael. *What Happens in Holy Communion?* Grand Rapids: Eerdmans, 2000.

Written by a contemporary Reformed theologian from Germany, this book is a fresh articulation of the meaning of the Lord's Supper. Welker explores classic resources in the Reformed tradition as well as the resources of ecumenical documents on Communion. The book is divided into twelve short chapters, each of which presents a central affirmation on the Lord's Supper and an issue that impacts pastoral ministry or justice concerns or ecumenical dialogue.

BAPTIST PERSPECTIVES

Cross, Anthony R., and Philip E. Thompson, eds. *Baptist Sacramentalism.* Carlisle, U.K.: Paternoster Press, 2003.

A collection of essays promoting a higher view of the sacraments (baptism, the Lord's Supper) than one normally associates with Baptist faith and practice.

Dodd, Monroe E. *Christ's Memorial*. Nashville: The Sunday School Board of the Southern Baptist Convention, 1934.

One of the few monographs on the Lord's Supper by a Baptist theologian. It covers all the major Baptist views while focusing especially on the traditional "Zwinglian" or memorialist view.

Lumpkin, W. L. *Baptist Confessions of Faith*. Valley Forge, Penn.: Judson Press, 1959.

A critical collection of Baptist statements of faith throughout the centuries and across denominations (conventions).

PENTECOSTAL PERSPECTIVES

Duffield, Guy P., and Nathaniel M. Van Cleave. *Foundations of Pentecostal Theology*, pp. 435-39. Los Angeles: L.I.F.E. Bible College, 1983.

These pages present a short, typical Pentecostal exposition of "ordinances," both water baptism and the Lord's Supper. That these well-known Pentecostal teachers and leaders devote less than five pages to the topic—in a book of more than 600 pages!—reflects the lack of interest among many Pentecostals in sacramentology.

Hollenweger, Walter J. *The Pentecostals*. London: SCM Press, 1972.

Chapter twenty-seven is a standard academic treatment of Pentecostal sacramentology by the leading international expert on global Pentecostalism. Furthermore, throughout the book that introduces Pentecostal movements all around the world, there are occasional references to the topic as well.

Hunter, Harold D. "Ordinances, Pentecostal." In *The New International Dictionary of Pentecostal and Charismatic Movements*, pp. 947-49. Edited by Stanley M. Burgess and Eduard M. van der Maas. Rev. and expanded ed. Grand Rapids: Zondervan, 2002.

A succinct, concise dictionary statement of both baptism and the Lord's Supper.

Kärkkäinen, Veli-Matti. "The Spirit and the Lord's Supper." In *Toward a Pneumatological Theology: Pentecostal and Ecumenical Perspectives on Ecclesiology, Soteriology, and Theology of Mission*, pp. 135-46. Edited by Amos Yong. Lanham, Md.: University Press of America, 2002.

Develops a theology of the Lord's Supper from a pneumatological perspective in critical dialogue with ecumenical and historical views.

Subject Index

Scripture Index